THE PAINLESS
VEGETARIAN

For Aeneas and Devona, two lifelong vegetarians – healthy and beautiful proof of the virtues of a vegetarian diet.

THE PENNILESS VEGETARIAN

OVER 100 MOUTH-WATERING MENUS

DAVID SCOTT

RIDER
LONDON • SYDNEY • AUCKLAND • JOHANNESBURG

First published in the UK in 1992 by Rider
An imprint of Random Century Group Ltd,
20 Vauxhall Bridge Road, London SW1V 2SA

Random Century Group Australia (Pty) Ltd,
20 Alfred Street, Milsons Point
Sydney, NSW 2061, Australia

Random Century New Zealand Ltd
18 Poland Road, Glenfield,
Auckland 10, New Zealand

Random Century Group South Africa (Pty) Ltd,
PO Box 337, Bergvlei 2012, South Africa

Typeset by 🅵🅰 Tek Art Ltd, Addiscombe, Croydon, Surrey
Printed and bound in Great Britain by
The Guernsey Press Co. Ltd, Guernsey, Channel Islands

The right of David Scott to be identified as
the author of this work has been asserted by him
in accordance with the Copyright, Designs and
Patents Act, 1988.

A catalogue record for this book is available from
the British Library.

ISBN 0 7126 5261 2

This book is printed on recycled paper.

This book contains material from previous David Scott publications.

CONTENTS

INTRODUCTION

The intention of this book is to show how we can make vegetarian meals to suit every occasion, that are not only healthy and delicious but also simple and cheap to prepare.

Vegetarians were once considered cranky, but nowadays there are many many people who for moral, health or economic reasons follow a vegetarian diet. The ethical reasons for doing so are for each individual to decide upon for themselves, but the nutritional benefits of a balanced vegetarian diet are well supported by current findings on what constitutes healthy eating.

Common nutritional defects in modern eating habits are usually caused by one or more of the following: too much fat, too much refined carbohydrate and sugar, too much salt, too many additives (found in processed foods), not enough vitamins and minerals and too little fibre. The simplest way to remedy any of these defects in the diet is to eat a wide variety of unrefined foods, especially vegetables (raw and cooked), grains, pulses and fruit, and to reduce the amount of all fats (including polyunsaturates) that we eat. The balanced vegetarian diet fulfils all these requirements and as an added bonus allows us to save money on our food bills. The average vegetarian spends between a third and one half less on food each week than a person who includes moderate amounts of meat and fish in their diet.

An interesting, healthy and varied vegetarian diet is possible even on a moderate budget. This means making your own meals from staple ingredients such as grains, beans and vegetables, which is far cheaper than buying expensive convenience foods and does ensure that you know what you are eating. It may be more time consuming, but it's surprising how quickly nutritious and delicious meals can be made once you have developed even a small repertoire of main dishes and a collection of soups and salads to go with them. Also with this style of cooking, there are usually sufficient leftovers to put together a quick lunch for the next day or to make a soup or casserole dish for the following evening meal.

Further, by adopting a diet which means eating more fresh vegetables, fruit, grains and wholemeal flour products, most of us will increase our carbohydrate intake and reduce the amount of protein we eat. This is a good thing since many of us (apart from children and pregnant women) eat far too much protein (and high protein foods such as meat and fish are expensive). It should be noted that carbohydrate foods contain no more calories than protein foods despite the common belief that they are more fattening.

This book is divided into two sections. The first section provides background nutritional and culinary information and the second gives a large selection of recipes. The chapters in the first section cover the following topics:- nutrition, with details of individual nutrients and how best to ensure we get them from the food we eat in the right amounts and combinations; general rules for a healthy diet; how to introduce the family to healthier, vegetarian foods; buying and cooking tips for each of the main vegetarian food groups, that is grains, pulses, vegetables, fruit, dairy products and nuts; stocking a store cupboard; basic kitchen equipment needs; and finally over 100 menu suggestions for a variety of meals ranging from breakfasts to dinner parties. The dishes given in these menus are cross-referenced with the recipes that appear in the second part of the book. The recipes here are collected under conventional headings such as starters, soups, salads, vegetable dishes and so on. Throughout the book the underlying theme will be the production of meals that are tasty, nutritious and economical to make.

NUTRITION

The combination of foods we eat, their quantity and their relative quantities to one another are important in a good vegetarian diet. We need to ensure that we have satisfactory amounts of proteins, carbohydrates, vitamins, minerals, fibre and fat, and that we maintain a balance between what we eat and the energy we expend. Otherwise we get too thin or too fat. Whole grains (such as in wholemeal bread and pasta, brown rice and unrefined breakfast cereals) eaten in combination with fresh and cooked vegetables and fruit, make an important contribution to a balanced diet. If, alongside these food groups, we include in our diet pulses, eggs, milk, yoghurt, cheeses, nuts and seeds, it will contain all the nutrients we require in satisfactory quantities, in the right combinations and be low in fat content.

The nutrients each of the food groups best provide are as follows:

Protein   whole grains, dairy produce, pulses, nuts and seeds and green vegetables (in small amounts, but of high quality)

Complex Carbohydrates   whole grains, fresh fruit and vegetables

Vitamins and Minerals   unrefined fresh foods of all types

Fibre   whole grains, fresh fruit and vegetables

Fats   unhydrogenated vegetable oils (where available cold pressed oils are the best)

For a healthy and energy-giving diet all five nutrient categories are needed in the right balance. Proteins are needed for growth, repair and maintenance of bodily tissues. Carbohydrates and fats provide energy for the body's activities and fats are also the source of the fat–soluble vitamins A, D, E and K. Vitamins and minerals are only required in very small amounts, but they are essential to the right functioning and the regulation of all the body's processes. Fibre is essential to the efficient elimination of waste products.

Protein

It used to be thought that without a 'good helping' of red meat we wouldn't get sufficient protein, but the truth is that most of us eat more than we need (excess is used as an energy source or goes to fat) and we can obtain our requirements comfortably from a varied vegetarian diet.

The main sources of protein in a lacto-vegetarian* diet are grains, pulses, milk, milk products, eggs, nuts and seeds. Eaten in the right quantity and combination these foods can provide protein of a very high quality, enough even for the needs of an energetic sports person, manual worker or growing child. Whole grains, pulses and vegetables also supply carbohydrates and proteins in correct complex proportions for good stamina. Many athletes, including the author, taking part in endurance events such as marathon running, have discovered that a diet based on these foods suits them well.

PROTEIN COMPLEMENTARITY

Although plant foods such as grains and beans are good sources of protein in their own right, many of them lack one or more of the essential amino acids which if present would give them a very high protein value. Fortunately, the amino acid in short supply in one plant food is often available in excess in another and vice versa. By combining two or more complementary plant foods in one meal we obtain protein of much higher quality or biological value than the sum total obtained from eating the foods separately. For example, most grains (e.g. rice, wheat, corn) or grain products are high in the amino acid tryptophan but low in lysine, while most pulses (e.g. beans, peas, lentils) are high in lysine and low in tryptophan. Thus a dish containing, say, rice and lentils will supply protein of a

*Throughout the book, when I say 'vegetarian' I mean a lacto-vegetarian, that is, someone who includes milk, milk products and eggs in their diet. I do not mean a vegan who relies solely on plant food for all nutritional needs.

higher biological value than the same total weight of rice or lentils on their own.

The combinations of food groups which advantageously complement their individual biological values are given below:

1   Milk, cheese, yoghurt or other milk products either in or with any dish containing grains, pulses, nuts or seeds
2   Grains either whole or as a flour product either in or with any dish containing pulses or dairy products
3   Pulses either in or with any dish containing grains, dairy products or nuts and seeds

Fats

Fats provide a concentrated energy source and the essential fat soluble vitamins A, D, E and K. Every fat or oil contains active (unsaturated) or inactive (saturated) acids or both. The active acids are called essential fatty acids (EFA). They are contained in the polyunsaturated fats recommended by many authorities over saturated fats as a precaution against heart disease. The saturated fats generally come from animal sources such as red meats, butter, cream or cheese. Thus it is healthier to use vegetable oils, such as sunflower, olive, safflower and sesame seed oils, polyunsaturated margarines and low-fat cheeses or other low-fat milk products in your cooking. I would also recommend that fats of any description be used in only moderate amounts, particularly saturated fats. There is now a considerable body of opinion that the risk of heart disease, high blood pressure and some cancers can be reduced by cutting saturated fat intake.

Note: If you do reduce the total fat content of your diet, there is no reason why you should not use butter sparingly, particularly if you enjoy it. Butter is a natural product, it contains no additives and is unprocessed. It is, however, a saturated fat.

Carbohydrates

Carbohydrates are the body's main source of energy. They are present in foods as starches and sugars. Starch is obtained from cereal grains and their products, pulses, vegetables (especially root vegetables) and nuts. The complex combination of starches and protein in these foods is a good one for people involved in manual work or sport. Naturally occurring sugars are found in fruit, honey and milk. Refined sugar, added liberally to so many foods, should be used moderately. Sugar is often thought of as being essential in providing us with energy, but in fact we can obtain all the energy we need from other more nutritious foods. Refined sugar provides only calories and contains no vitamins, minerals or protein and it displaces other more nutritious foods from our diets.

Most of us, however, have a liking for sweet things and this tends to stay with us throughout our lives. Thus we need to exercise some control over the amount of sweet foods, such as cakes, chocolate and puddings we eat and to gradually wean ourselves off adding spoonfuls of sugar to things like tea, coffee and breakfast cereal – and to choose cereals which have no added sugar.

Fibre

Fibre is found in unrefined cereals, fruit and vegetables. It is not a nutrient because it is not digested, but because it adds bulk to the body's waste products, it is essential to efficient elimination.

Vitamins and Minerals

Vitamins and minerals in the right quantities and combinations are vital to our good health. The best way to obtain them is

MAIN VITAMINS IN BASIC FOOD GROUPS

GRAINS	LEGUMES	NUTS/SEEDS	VEGETABLES Green leafy	VEGETABLES Other	FRUIT	DAIRY	EGGS
B_1	B_1		A			A	
B_3	B_3	B_3	B_2	B_1		B_2	
B_5		B_5	B_5	B_5			
B_6		B_6	B_6 (some)	B_6 (some)		B_6 (some)	B_6 (some)
BIOTIN		BIOTIN			BIOTIN		BIOTIN
	FOLIC ACID		FOLIC ACID			B_{12}	
				C	C (Citrus fruit)		
						D	D (yolk)
E		E	E veg. oils also			E	E

through the food we eat. The best diet to ensure we get a good supply of them is one that includes a wide variety of unprocessed foods. Thus, as mentioned several times already, we need to eat plenty of fresh vegetables, fruit, whole grain and flour products and to a lesser extent pulses and dairy products. Vitamin and mineral levels generally drop in foods if they are stored for too long or overcooked. The highest levels occur in raw foods, such as in vegetables and fruits. The main vitamins and minerals occurring in the basic vegetarian food groups are shown in the tables on pages 12 and 14. Vitamins and minerals of specific interest are discussed below.

VITAMIN C

If you are under stress or ill or living on a poor diet, then vitamin and mineral supplements may be important, but normally we should not require more nutrients than those found naturally in our food. One possible exception to this general rule is Vitamin C.

We live in a polluted environment and because our food is often unavoidably dosed with pesticides and additives, we absorb, and produce metabolically, an unnatural amount and number of oxidising agents in the form of free radicals. Free radical activity in the body has been associated (not yet proven conclusively) with a number of illnesses, including cancer. Fortunately Vitamin C has the quality of mopping up these agents and neutralizing them. A number of nutritionists are now recommending, in view of these findings, that we increase our Vitamin C intake to at least 150mg per day or higher.

VITAMIN B_{12}

Vitamin B_{12} is found almost exclusively in foods of animal origin. If you include dairy products in your diet, you will obtain sufficient B_{12} for your needs. For vegans non-animal sources of B_{12} are miso (fermented soya bean paste), brewers yeast (available in tablet form), sea kelp, soya milk and yeast

MAIN MINERALS IN BASIC FOOD GROUPS

	GRAINS	LEGUMES	NUTS/SEEDS	VEGETABLES Green leafy	VEGETABLES Other	FRUIT	DAIRY/EGGS
Zn–Zinc Se–Selenium	Zn Se (wheatgerm) (bran)	Zn	Zn	Se (some)	Se (some)		
K–Potassium Mn–Manganese	Mn	K	K Mn	K Mn	K Mn (moderate amount)	K Mn (moderate amount)	K
Cu–Copper Cr–Chromium	Cr	Cu	Cu	Cu Cr	Cr	Cr (fair)	Cr (cheese)
Ca–Calcium	Ca	Ca (especially tofu)		Ca			Ca
Fe–Iron Mg–Magnesium	Fe Mg	Fe Mg	Fe Mg	Fe Mg	Mg		

extracts, such as Barmene and Tastex. Draught beer from the cask also contains B_{12}. Two pints is equal to the daily need for B_{12}.

IRON

Most of the nutrients that meat provides can be obtained from other foods, with perhaps the exception of iron. Iron is needed to make sufficient haemoglobin, which is the oxygen carrying protein present in red blood cells. If we do not have enough of this, we become anaemic. The iron from meat, including poultry, is better absorbed than the iron from other foods but as the body gets used to eating less meat, it increases its efficiency in absorbing iron from foods like bread and flour, green vegetables, eggs and pulse vegetables. The absorption is helped further if these foods and a good source of Vitamin C are eaten at the same meal. (e.g. include a salad and/or fresh fruit and/or green vegetables with each meal).

GENERAL RULES FOR A HEALTHY DIET

A varied diet of natural foods, composed mainly of whole grains or whole grain products, fresh vegetables and fruits, dried (not tinned) pulses, unhydrogenated vegetable oils, nuts, seeds and dairy products in moderation, will supply all the nutrients you need. Natural foods taste better than refined foods and their nutrient and fibre content is always higher. A diet composed mainly of refined foods, often full of sugar and additives, saturated fats and too much salt, is definitely bad for your health. However, having said that, it does no harm to eat a slice of white bread or have more cream than you really need just occasionally. Moderation and self-awareness of your own needs are the touchstones of a good diet and an obsession with proper eating, like an obsession with overeating, causes tension and bad digestion.

As a general guide, the main meal of the day should provide approximately 50 per cent of the protein you need, one light meal should provide about 25 per cent and breakfast about 25 per cent. Each meal should contain two or more major protein sources and at least one meal should include two or more lightly cooked fresh vegetables and a fresh salad (including a leafy green vegetable). Fresh fruit (including citrus fruits), three or four times a day, completes the day's requirements.

Snacks

Snack foods in particular are frequently too sweet, too fatty or too salty and they are sometimes rightly described as junk food. Where possible avoid the popular commercial snacks and substitute natural foods, which, as I have already said, taste better and have much higher nutrient and fibre contents. One word of caution – many manufacturers, aware that whole foods are now more popular, tag the words healthy, whole or wholesome onto the most awful concoctions, so always look at the ingredients carefully.

Fresh fruit is the most obvious snack food. Fruit in season, thoroughly washed, is usually the best-tasting and cheapest. Dried fruit such as apricots, figs, bananas and dates are also convenient. Nuts, singly or mixed, preferably unsalted, are nutritious and filling. Many wholefood and health shops now sell snack mixes such as trail-mix, Bombay-mix, tropical fruit-mix etc. These are usually good, especially if mixed and packed in the shop. Wholemeal bread with cheese and green salad is an excellent snack. Muesli with fruit and yoghurt is not just a breakfast food. It can quickly and healthily fill a mid-morning or mid-afternoon gap. Finally, familiar dishes such as cheese on toast or beans on toast made with wholemeal bread, spread with a good cold-pressed vegetable oil margarine are fine stand-bys for a quick meal.

INTRODUCING THE FAMILY TO HEALTHIER AND VEGETARIAN FOODS

Introducing vegetarian and healthier foods into family eating is not always easy and I hope this book offers some help. In conjunction with the book, one way to start is to serve nutritious vegetarian dishes that are already familiar more often. For instance, baked potatoes with cottage cheese, beans on toast, omelettes, wholemeal pasta with olive oil (or cheese) and black pepper, wholemeal bread or toast with peanut butter and slices of raw vegetables with a mayonnaise dip are all nutritionally sound and more so if served with a simple salad. Then slowly introduce onto the menu new vegetarian dishes from the selection given in this book.

For those absolutely new to vegetarianism, start to slowly reduce meat intake by, for example, reducing the meat in casserole dishes and adding instead more vegetables or lentils or grains, like rice or bulgar wheat or couscous. Serve main course salads and side salads more often and for desserts sometimes offer fruit or fruit salads in place of puddings or cakes. For snacks try nuts and raisins in place of biscuits or crisps and fruit in place of sweets (see page 17 for more snack ideas). Also begin to nutritionally improve favourite family dishes by, for instance, reducing the fat or oil (change animal fats for vegetable) and sugar used in their recipes or use unrefined ingredients like wholemeal flour in place of refined foods such as white flour.

One final suggestion for new adherents to a vegetarian diet. Avoid making a fuss about it. The subject can become very boring for other people, particularly firmly established carnivores and long-standing vegetarians.

BUYING AND COOKING NOTES

Grains & Pasta

There are many thousands of species of grains, of which only a dozen or more comprise the world's principal cereal crops. These provide the staple foods for most of the world's population, since cereal grains, either whole or as flour products, are excellent, well-balanced, complete sources of nutrients. Until quite recently particular grains were associated with particular areas of the world. For instance, wheat with Europe, maize (corn) with the Americas and rice with much of Asia. Nowadays these divisions are not so well defined and the ordinary cook in Britain or America has a whole range of grains to choose from. General rules for cooking a variety of grains and a number of culinary tips on ways to use them are given on pages 24 and 25.

The main grains used in Western cooking are as follows:

BARLEY

Whole barley or *pot barley* is more nutritious than the refined pearl barley, but it takes longer to cook. It is mainly used in soups, stews and casseroles.

BUCKWHEAT

Not strictly a grain but the seed of a herbaceous plant, buckwheat is popular in Russia and other Eastern European countries. The grain, or *kasha* as it is also called, looses some of its flavour if it is not dry roasted before cooking. Buy pre-roasted buckwheat or dry roast the plain variety before boiling it. Kasha has an interesting nutty flavour. It is good served on its own or an an ingredient in savoury dishes and patties. Crushed buckwheat and buckwheat flour are used in pancake and muffin batters.

CORN (maize)

Five varieties of corn are grown commercially but only two, corn on the cob and dent corn (from which cornmeal is ground), are of interest to the cook. Wholegrain maize or cornmeal retains all the goodness of the corn. Stoneground is the best if you can obtain it. *Polenta* is the Italian name for yellow maize or cornmeal. It is a staple food in parts of northern Italy where boiled polenta, cooked and then fired sometimes takes the place of bread. Cornflour is not as nutritious as whole maize flour, but excellent for thickening soups, sauces etc.

MILLET

In the West, millet is generally demoted to animal food, but why this is so is a mystery. Nutritionally millet compares well with other cereals and the cooked grains and flours are delicious. It contains vitamins of the B complex, important minerals (especially iron) and 9 per cent by weight of protein. Millet grain is hulled since the outer part is too hard to cook. Fortunately this does not involve a large nutrient loss and millet grain is almost as nutritious as whole millet flour which includes the milled hull or bran section of the grain. Many peoples with long life-expectancy, including the famous Hunzas of the Himalayas, cultivate millet as a staple crop.

OATS

Oats are a rich source of nutrients. They are usually used only in breakfast cereals, but can also be added to soups, stews and other savoury dishes. Oatmeal flour is used in bread and cake making. Oats are traditionally the main ingredient of *muesli*, which was formulated by the Swiss nutritionist Dr Bircher-Benner over 70 years ago. The recipe was devised to provide a dish that supplied good amounts of protein, vitamins, minerals and roughage without overloading the body with too much rich food. Muesli is considered by most nutritionists to be an excellent food combination.

RICE

Rice is an excellent food for the cook. It is versatile and adaptable and once you have learned to judge how to cook it well, you can produce good plain boiled rice and rice combination dishes without fail. Before it is cooked, rice should be washed. American or European packed rice only needs a light rinse, but loose rice or Asian packed rice should be rinsed in a colander until the water stops running milky. Once rice has been washed before cooking, it is not necessary to do so again afterwards. If cooked rice needs a lot of draining through using too much cooking water, you will lose nutrients and flavour with the drained water.

Brown rice is more nutritious than white rice and if you enjoy the flavour of it and also have the extra time needed to cook it, then you will benefit from including it in your diet. If you prefer white rice, as some people do, then make sure the rest of your diet is well mixed and that it includes fruit and vegetables for the fibre.

Long grain rice (often called patna rice since it was thought to have originated from Patna in India) remains in separate grains and becomes light and fluffy when cooked. It is excellent for serving on its own as well as in pilavs, paellas etc. Short grain rices are soft when cooked and the grains tend to stick gently to one another. For savoury dishes, except in Japan, parts of China and in Italy for making risottos, most people prefer long grain rice. Short grain rice is generally used for desserts. The pudding rice we use to make rice pudding is a short grain variety. Incidentally, wild rice is a cereal grain native to North

America, China and Japan. It is in the same broad family as the rice plant, but it has never been domestically cultivated. Raw wild rice is brown but it acquires a faint purplish colour when cooked. It has a delicate nutty flavour.

WHEAT AND WHEAT PRODUCTS

There are numerous ways of cooking wheat and wheat flour products. The variety of cooking methods has, of course, resulted from regional differences, the types of wheat available, cultural traditions, the influence of technology and, not least, human inventiveness.

Brown and White Bread   To get the best nutritional value out of wheat, we should buy or make bread from 100 per cent wholemeal flour milled on stone rollers. This does not take the question of taste or appetite into account however, and on occasions we may prefer a lighter, blander-tasting but less nutritious bread than the wholemeal variety. Who, for instance, can resist a freshly baked French loaf?

The nutritional qualities of different breads are illustrated in the chart below, which shows the nutrient content of flours of various extraction rates. White bread is made from flour of 65 per cent to 70 per cent extraction, and brown breads from flours of 80 per cent to 100 per cent extraction.

NUTRITIONAL CONTENT OF FLOURS OF DIFFERENT EXTRACTION RATES

Type of flour	Protein	Fibre	Carbo-hydrate (gm per 100 gm flour)	B_1	B_2	Niacin	Iron	Calcium (mg per 100 gm flour)
100% (wholemeal flour)	12·2	2·00	64·1	0·37	0·12	5·70	3·50	36·0
81% (brown bread)	11·7	0·21	70·2	0·24	0·06	1·60	1·65	–
70%	11·3	0·10	72·0	0·08	0·05	0·80	1·25	–

Bulgar Wheat   This is parboiled, cracked wheat. Although relatively unknown in the west, bulgar wheat is the staple food of several Middle Eastern countries, where it is served with rice and also used as the basis for a variety of cold salads. Bulgar has all the nutritional qualities of wholewheat grain. It has a distinctive taste and is easy to cook.

Semolina (couscous)   Semolina is produced from the starchy endosperm of the wheat grain. It is milled in various grades to give fine, medium or coarse semolina. Fine semolina is used in puddings and pasta production, while coarse semolina is used to make *couscous*.

Couscous is probably the most common and most widely known North African Arab dish in which the grains are steamed over a rich sauce or stew and then served in a mountainous heap with the sauce or stew poured over. Couscous is never cooked in the sauce. Traditionally the stew is made with mutton or chicken, though a vegetable variation is just as tasty. A special pot called a couscousier is traditionally used for cooking the stew and simultaneously steaming the couscous, but a saucepan with a snug-fitting colander on top will serve just as well.

Pasta   Italian style pasta is made from a dough of wheat flour, eggs and water. The dough is rolled out and cut into any of a huge variety of shapes, then dried before cooking in water. The best pasta is made from hard grained wheats, particularly durum wheat.

Wholewheat pasta is more nutritious and is higher in protein than normal white flour pasta.

When cooking pasta the important rule is to use a large pot and plenty of water. Generally 1 lb (450 g) pasta needs 6 pints (3 litres) water. For salt, 1½ tablespoons (22.5 ml) per 1 lb (450 g) pasta is an average amount, added after the water has boiled and before the pasta is put in. To prevent the pasta sticking to itself during cooking, a little butter or oil is added to the water. Thus, the water is brought to a rolling boil, salted, about 2 tablespoons (30 ml) oil are added and the pasta is then carefully fed into the pot and boiled, uncovered, until it is soft on the outside but with a slight resistance at the centre – *al dente*.

Cooking times vary depending on the type of pasta and whether it is bought or homemade. As soon as the pasta is cooked, drain it in a colander and serve with a sauce or grated cheese or on its own with olive oil and freshly milled black pepper.

GENERAL RULES FOR COOKING GRAINS

Rinse the grains under cold water and drain. Measure the cooking water into the pot and bring to the boil. Add the grain, stir, add salt if you wish (almost ¼–½ teaspoon to 8 oz (225 g) grains) and return the pot to the boil. Reduce heat to very low. Cover the pot and cook until the water is absorbed and the grain is tender.

Cooking tips
1   Do not stir grains during cooking; it makes them sticky.
2   For a change sauté the grains with some chopped onion in a little oil before adding the cooking water. It changes their flavour.
3   Cook lentils and brown rice together.
4   Combine left-over grains with beans, add dressing and chopped salad vegetables.
5   Add herbs or spices to the grain cooking water.
6   Sprinkle cooked grains with roasted nuts or seeds.
7   Replace grain cooking water with stock.

COOKING GRAINS

Grain	Water to grain ratio	Cooking time	Comments
Barley (whole)	3:1	1 hour	Cooked whole barley is used as you would use rice. Pearl barley is suitable only for soups and puddings.
Buckwheat	2:1	15–20 minutes	Better known as *kasha* which is roasted buckwheat. Nutty flavour, makes good flour mixed with wheat flour. It is the seed of a herbaceous plant and not truly a grain.

Grain	Water to grain ratio	Cooking time	Comments
Bulgar Wheat	2:1	15–20 minutes	Also known as burghul, prepared by parboiling wholewheat grains, drying and cracking them. Contains all the goodness of wholewheat. Cooks quickly. Good dry roasted before boiling.
Millet	3:1	40–45 minutes	Light yellow millet with small spherical grains most popular in Britain. Use in place of rice. Often enjoyed by children more than rice. Nutritionally balanced.
Rice White Brown	2:1 2:1	15–20 minutes 50 mins to 1 hr	Rice is the world's most important food crop. Brown rice is excellent nutritionally, although white rice is more favoured since it is less chewy and cooks more quickly. Long and medium grain rice is best for savoury dishes. Short grain rice is stickier and better for puddings.
Wholewheat berries (cracked wheat	3:1 2:1	1½–2 hours 20–25 minutes)	Takes a lot of cooking, remains quite fibrous but tasty and filling. Makes good salads. Berries cracked for quicker cooking. Use in place of rice.
Wild rice	3:1	1 hour	Lovely plant grown in fresh water in America, China and Japan. Brown with faint purplish colour when cooked. Delicate, nutty flavour.
Couscous	Enough to cover	20–30 minutes Usually sold precooked, so no need to boil; just steam or soak in hot water for time given above.	Wheat grain product made from semolina. Convenient alternative to rice and main grain served in North Africa.

Beans

The seeds of the plants of the legume or pulse family are generally described as beans. This includes beans, peas and lentils. Baked and cooked properly they are a versatile, tasty, economical and nutritious protein food. Beans are particularly rich in the B vitamins, thiamine and niacin, and the minerals, calcium and iron. Sprouted beans are also high in Vitamin C. Combined with grains they provide an excellent protein source.

Store beans in a dry, cool place in airtight containers. They come in many fascinating and attractive shapes and colours so, if you can, store them in glass containers on open shelves. Before cooking beans check them for any small stones or grit. This is especially necessary with lentils.

Beans contain two starches which are difficult to digest if they are not broken down before eating. For this reason it is essential that they are well pre-soaked and cooked for the correct time before consumption. This particularly applies to kidney beans which also contain a harmful substance destroyed only by correct cooking. The long soaking required does mean you have to remember to do it in advance of the meal. The usual soaking times are 12 to 24 hours, although there is a quicker method which is discussed below. Strictly speaking lentils and split peas do not require soaking, but if you do soak them it doesn't do any harm and speeds up the cooking time.

Soaking Method

Weigh out the beans you require – 8 oz (225 g) serves about 4 people. Pick over to remove any grit or stones or odd-looking beans. Cover the beans in cold water – 2 pints (1.1 litre) per 8 oz (225 g) beans. Leave according to the recommended soaking times (long method) given in the chart on pages 28 and 29. If the beans are cooked in the water they are soaked in, the water will be almost completely absorbed by the end of the cooking time and the beans will not need to be drained. This method preserves any vitamins lost in the water. Of course, more water may be added during the cooking as necessary. If you forget or need to leave the beans longer than the recommended soaking time, then they should be drained and covered with fresh water before cooking.

Quick Soaking Method
If you forget to put the beans in to soak, here is a quick method. In a heavy saucepan weigh out the beans and cover with water as directed in the standard soaking method. Cover the pot and bring to the boil, reduce the heat and simmer for five minutes. Now remove the pot from the heat and leave the beans to soak for the short method time given in the chart on pages 28 and 29. Then bring the beans to the boil in the same water and cook until tender. Cooking times are the same as for the long soaking method.

Pressure Cooking
Pressure cooking, if carried on too long, reduces the flavour of the beans and makes them mushy. We recommend it only if you are in a rush. Times are given in the chart on pages 28 and 29.

Cooking Tips
1   Do not add salt to the beans until near the end of the cooking time, otherwise they harden and take longer to cook.
2   Other seasoning should be added later as well, since cooking beans seems to absorb and neutralise flavours. Lentils and split peas are the exception to this rule and can be seasoned at the start of cooking.
3   If a bean dish is to be reheated the following day, check the seasoning and add more if necessary before serving.
4   Do not add bicarbonate of soda to the cooking water. It's not needed and destroys vitamins.
5   Do not discard any water in which beans have been cooked as it makes excellent stock.
6   Chickpeas and red beans tend to foam when first cooked. Remove the scum after 20 or 30 minutes and again later if any more forms.
7   Cook twice as many beans as you need and store the extra in the fridge until needed. I find they keep best if only lightly covered. They will keep for 4 to 5 days. Use for making soups, salads, spreads, dips, mashed for rissoles, combined

COOKING BEANS

Beans	Soaking times long method hours	Soaking times short method hours	Cooking times without pressure hours	Cooking times with pressure[1] mins	Comments
Aduki beans	2–3	1	1–1½	8–10	Small pod, sweetish, easy to digest. Called King of Beans in Japan.
Black beans	8–12	3	1½–2	10–15	Black, shiny. Popular in Caribbean. Good in soups, casseroles.
Black-eyed beans	8–12	2	1–1½	8–10	White or creamy with black or dark yellow eye. 'Soul food' in America.
Broad beans	8–12	4	1½–2	10–15	Creamy white and brown. Popular in casseroles and salads.
Lima/butter beans	8–12	4	1½–2	10–15	Long soaking essential. White and brown varieties. Good in soups, casseroles and salads.
Chickpeas	8–12	3	1½–2	10–15	Also called garbanzos. Yellow with dimpled surface. Popular in Middle Eastern cuisine. Main ingredient in hummus.
Kidney beans including: Egyptian brown beans (ful medames)	8–12	2–3	1½–2	10–15	Tasty, main ingredient in Fue, the Egyptian national dish. Cooked with cumin, seasoned with garlic, lemon and oil.
Great northern bean	8–12	2–3	1½–2	10–15	Large white beans, popular cooked, then baked. Good in stews and casseroles.
Haricot beans	8–12	2–3	1½–2	10–15	Used to make the ubiquitous baked beans in

Navy beans	8–12	2–3	1–1½	10–15	Small white bean, very similar in taste and use to haricot bean.
Pinto bean	8–12	2–3	1–1½	10–15	Beige colour with speckles. Popular in Mexican cuisine. Turns brown when cooked.
Red kidney bean	8–12	2–3	1–1½	10–15	Very popular flavoursome beans. Used to make chilli. Good in salads.
Lentils	no soaking needed		small: 20–30 mins large: 35–45 mins	6–10	Red, brown or green. Most popular in soups, or as dahl (lentils cooked with onion, spices and garlic). Red variety sold split for quick cooking. Cooked with rice, brown lentils make a good pilav dish, nutritious and tasty.
Mung beans	8–12	45–60 mins	45 mins	10	Also called green gram. Grows quickly. Excellent for growing bean sprouts.
Pigeon peas	8–12	2	1	10	Small round flat peas, speckled with brown marks. Popular in Caribbean, where they are eaten with rice.
Peas	8–12	2	1	10	Common pea or garden pea. Sold fresh or dried.
Split peas	no soaking needed		20–30 min	6–10	Good in soups and stews. Famous in pease pudding.
Soya beans	24	do not use this method	3–4	30	Most nutritious of all beans. They need lots of soaking and cooking. Best eaten as TVP or beancurd or miso[2]. Genuine soya sauce is made from fermented soya beans.

[1] 15 lb pressure cooker   [2] See section on soya bean products

with cooked grains or as an accompaniment to a main meal.

8   One volume of dried beans gives 2–2½ volumes of cooked beans. One weight of dried beans gives 2–2½ weights of cooked beans. Thus, 1 cup of dried beans yields 2–2½ cups cooked beans and 8 oz (225 g) dried beans gives 1–1¼ lb (450 g–675 g) cooked beans.

SOYA BEAN PRODUCTS

Miso   A fermented soya bean and grain product, it has a thick consistency and is usually dark coloured with a pungent smell. Miso is rich in vitamins (including B_{12}) and minerals and is good for settling the digestive system. It can be used in soups, stews, stocks, sauces, dressings, dips and spreads, but is salty and care should be taken not to add extra salt. Miso keeps unrefrigerated for months.

Soya Flour   Special heat-treated soya-flour, such as Soyolk, can be used uncooked, e.g in making vegan 'cheese'.

Soya Milk   This is made from boiled, crushed soya beans, and used by vegans in place of cow's milk. It is high in protein and low in fat. Soya milk is available commercially in health and wholefood stores. Buy fresh rather than canned milk (Plamil is a well-known brand).

Soya Sauce   Soya sauce is an all-purpose seasoning used to highlight the individual flavour of all the ingredients in the dish to which it is added. It should not be used to drown the flavour of food. Correctly made, soya sauce is prepared from the liquid residue collected in the miso making process or from soya beans fermented specially for soya sauce production. It is not related to the artificially flavoured, chemical filled liquid found in many bottles claiming to be soya sauce. *Shoyu* is soya sauce made from a fermented soya bean and wheat mixture while *tamari* is made only from soya beans and is gluten free.

Tempeh   Tempeh is made by culturing split soya beans with a mould such as *rhizopus oligusporus*. The beans break down and bind together forming a firm cake with a white skin similar to that found on some French cheeses. The texture of tempeh ranges from soft to crunchy and the taste is slightly nutty. Tempeh is an excellent source of protein, vitamins, carbohydrates and minerals and it is an important nutritional food in South East Asia. Tempeh is just becoming available in the better stocked wholefood shops. It's worth trying if you can find a stockist.

Tofu (also called beancurd) This is made by boiling soya beans, mashing the boiled beans through a sieve and collecting the liquid or milk, which is then set using a coagulant. Excess water is pressed off. Fresh tofu is best kept in water. Vacuum-packed tofu is also available. Tofu is rich in protein and minerals and low in fat. It is a versatile food and may be used in soups, stews, salads, dips, dressings or stir-fried with vegetables. It may even be used in sweet dishes (cheesecake for instance) as a substitute for cheese.

Home-made beancurd
Cover 1 lb (450 g) soya beans with water and leave to soak for at least 12 hours. Change the water once during soaking. Drain and grind the beans either in an electric grinder or hand mill. Transfer to a heavy pan and add 2½ times as much water by volume as beans. Bring to the boil, reduce heat and simmer for 1 hour. Arrange three to four layers of cheesecloth inside a colander placed over a large bowl or pan. Strain the bean mixture through this. Finally, gather the cheesecloth around the collected bean pulp and squeeze out as much of the remaining liquid into the bowl or pan as possible. Transfer the collected liquid to a glass bowl. Add 3 tablespoons (45 ml) fresh lemon juice to it, stir once, cover with a damp cloth and leave in a warm spot – 80°F (120°C) is perfect – for 8–12 hours or until the beancurd sets. Drain through cheesecloth to remove excess liquid. The beancurd may now be used. For a professional look, pour it into a square mould, put a light weight on top and press for 4 hours. Store under water in a refrigerator.

For flavoured beancurd, simmer a block or small squares of it in oil and soya sauce with mint, garlic, nutmeg, cinnamon, cloves, fennel or black pepper, or whatever seasoning you wish.

T.V.P. Textured vegetable protein (T.V.P.) is extracted from soya beans. It is made into meat substitute chunks or other meat replacement foods.

BEANSPROUTS

When beans or other seeds, such as alfalfa, are sprouted their nutritional value increases. During the sprouting process the dormant seed germinates and starts to grow and its B complex and Vitamin C content increases, amino acids are produced, fats are converted into water-soluble compounds and enzyme activity increases. Fresh beansprouts thus contain many of the nutrients lost from other foods during cooking and so make a healthy addition to a diet otherwise based on cooked or processed meals. (Francis Chichester supplemented his diet with beansprouts during his round-the-world boat trip aboard Gypsy Moth. He designed a special compartment in the galley for sprouting.) The other great advantages of beansprouts are that they are quick, simple and cheap to grow and available all year round.

Mung beansprouts are the most popular commercial variety and the beansprouts we are most familiar with in Chinese restaurant dishes. Other non-commercial favourites are sprouted chickpeas, kidney beans, soya beans and lentils. Mixtures of beans may also be sprouted to add variety to the taste and texture of beansprout dishes. Aduki beans, lentils, chickpeas and mung beans is a popular mix. Whole grains like rice, wheat and oats can also be sprouted, but they should be briefly cooked by stir-frying or steaming before eating. Fenugreek, alfalfa, sunflower and sesame seeds all sprout well and are delicious fresh or gently cooked.

Apart from fresh in salads or sandwiches and cooked in stir-fry dishes, beansprouts are good in soups and casseroles, wrapped in thin pastry sheets (as in spring rolls) or gently chopped in a food processor and added to bread dough before baking.

To sprout beans, grains or seeds (general method)

Place 1–2 oz (25–50 g) of beans, grains or seeds on the bottom of a large wide jar and half-fill it with water. The sprouts will be 6 times as bulky as the unsprouted beans, so make sure the jar is large enough – 1 oz (25 g) beans will make approximately 8 oz (225 g) beansprouts. Leave them to soak overnight and then drain the water away. Rinse the beans and drain again. A piece of cheesecloth placed over the mouth of the jar makes this job easy.

Now place the jar in a warm, dark place – about 70°F (20°C). Repeat the rinse and drain procedure 3 times a day for 3–5 days. The length of time before the sprouts are ready depends on the bean used and upon the stage at which you decide to harvest them. After this time mung beansprouts will be about 2 in (5 cm) long, while sprouts from chickpeas, lentils, kidney beans and soya beans will be ½ in (1 cm) long.

Spread the beansprouts (drained) on a tray in the daylight (indoors) for 2–3 hours. They can now be used as required. Store unused beansprouts in a covered container in the refrigerator and rinse before serving. They can be used fresh for up to 3 days or cooked for up to 5 days after harvesting.

If you have two jars available for bean sprouting you will have a constant source of fresh beansprouts available. Scald used cloths and jars before re-using to avoid spoiling the next batch.

SUGGESTIONS FOR SPROUTING

(approximate amount to use per batch)

Legumes	**Grains**	**Seeds**
4 oz (100g)	*3 tablespoons*	*(see each seed)*
Aduki beans	Barley	Alfalfa *(1 tablespoon)*
Broad beans	Corn	Fenugreek *(3 tablespoons)*
Chickpeas	Millet	Sesame *(3 tablespoons)*
Haricot beans	Oats	Sunflower *(6 tablespoons)*
Kidney beans	Rice	
Lentils	Rye	
Mung beans	Wheat	

Vegetables and Fruit

One of the essentials of good and economic cooking and healthy eating is to choose ingredients at their best. This is particularly so for fruit and vegetables. One way of contributing towards this is to buy in season and to select produce from farms and orchards as close to home as possible. In this way you will be buying fruit and vegetables at their freshest and cheapest. Remember also to take particular advantage of the flavoursome, short season crops such as soft fruits. Shopping for basics in this manner then leaves you with the freedom to occasionally buy and enjoy some of the wide range of exotic fruits and vegetables now being imported into Britain.

Always wash vegetables thoroughly and where suitable give them a good scrub. Peel them only if strictly necessary, since the skin contains many nutrients and is often tasty. As a basic rule cook vegetables in the minimum of time and water needed. The intention is always to ensure they retain their colour and texture.

SEASONAL BUYING

Below are general details of which fruits and vegetables, both home grown and imported, are particularly worth looking out for in each season. The lists are by no means comprehensive and do not include items generally available all year round such as mushrooms and beansprouts. They are a guide to good buys, but note that these will change in time as export and import markets change. If sometimes speed or the wish to make a particular dish is more important than cost, then of course you will buy what you want as long as it is available.

Spring Asparagus, avocados, baby white turnips, bananas, calabrese, chicory, citrus fruits, cucumbers, curly endive, courgettes, green beans, mangetout peas, mint, new potatoes, parsley, pineapples, radishes, spinach beet, tomatoes, watercress.

Summer All types of lettuce, apples, aubergines, beetroot, broad beans, broccoli, carrots, cauliflower, celery, corn on the cob, courgettes, French beans, garden peas, garlic, globe artichokes, Italian fennel, Italian plum tomatoes, kidney beans, peppers, runner beans, Spanish onions, tomatoes, watercress.

Autumn All root crops, apples, avocados, basil, cabbage (drumhead), celery, chicory, chillies, Chinese cabbage, courgettes, cucumbers, endive, fennel, flageolet beans, French beans, fresh dates, grapes, kiwi fruit, pomegranates, red pepper, runner beans, shallots, spinach, sweet corn, tomatoes, watercress.

Winter Avocados, beetroot, carrots, calabrese, cauliflower, celery, chicory, coriander, courgettes, endive, French beans, leeks, lemons, lettuce (Iceberg or Cos), mangetout peas, new potatoes, oranges, parsley, potatoes, purple/white broccoli, red/white cabbage.

HOW BEST TO COOK YOUR FRUIT AND VEGETABLES

Root Vegetables Carrots, potatoes and the like are best cooked at a fast simmer/slow boil. You want to cook the vegetables swiftly to retain as much flavour as possible, but you don't want to have the heat so high that the water is violently agitated, causing the outer parts of the vegetables to disintegrate before the food is cooked at the centre.

For best results, place the root vegetables in three times their volume of cold water, place the lid on the pan and bring swiftly to the boil. Then reduce heat and cook until tender.

Green Vegetables Green beans, broccoli and other green vegetables, are exceptional in that they are best cooked in an open pan at a furious boil. The reason is this. These vegetables contain substances which under the action of heat act to change the vegetable from bright green to a cheerless khaki colour. Fortunately the chemicals are volatile and if you can drive them off and out of the pan before they have a chance to act, your vegetables will remain green. You must then serve these vegetables immediately or, if they are for a salad, chill them under a cold tap or plunge them into iced water until they are quite cold.

When cooking in this manner note the following points:

1   The vegetables are normally cooked in salted water because the salt raises the temperature of boiling water a little, allowing the offending substances to be driven off a little more efficiently.

2   Have only ½ in (1.5 cm) to ¾ in (2 cm) water in your pan. There should not be enough water in the pan for the vegetables to charge around and break themselves up.

3   Have the water at a furious boil before you put in the green vegetables and maintain it that way.

4   Use a large-based pan and do not overcrowd. It will not matter if parts of your vegetables protrude, but they must all be in close proximity to the boiling water.

Tender Leaf Vegetables   Vegetables such as spinach are best cooked by washing well, shaking off the excess water and cooking without any additional water over moderate heat, in a covered pan.

Fruit   You should whenever possible try to eat much of your fruit raw to take full advantatge of its abundant Vitamin C. If you cook it, keep the cooking to a minimum, to retain as much Vitamin C as possible.

Fruit is traditionally cooked by poaching in a sugar syrup. The slow cooking prevents the fruit from breaking up and the strong sugar solution prevents the fruit flavours and natural sugars leaching away, as would happen if you cooked the fruit in water.

Poaching fruit in syrup may preserve the flavour, but at the expense of consuming hefty doses of sugar. Rather than poaching (or stewing in even the minimum of water), try baking fruit or steaming it whole in its skin. For example, wash pears well and place complete in a steamer basket. Cook the fruit until just soft, allow it to cool, peel it with a sharp knife, then slice in half and remove core with a teaspoon. Stuff the pear halves or cut them into segments.

DRIED FRUITS

Dried fruits are a very useful ingredient in the vegetarian diet. As long as you remember to soak those that need it ahead of time, dried fruits are an excellent ready-to-use ingredient in muesli and other breakfast cereals, in dried and fresh fruit salads, in savoury stuffings, casseroles, rice dishes, soups and sauces. They are nourishing and versatile foods and contain all the goodness of fresh fruit in a concentrated form. Dried fruits are generally rich in vitamins, minerals and energy giving sugars (which are much less tooth decaying than ordinary refined sugar) and they contain small amounts of protein.

Traditionally the fruits most often dried have been dates, grapes (as raisins, currants and sultanas), figs, plums (as prunes) and apricots. More recently dried apples, bananas, pears and even peaches have become popular. A whole range of dried fruits, either individually or in mixed bags, is available in health food stores and better supermarkets. Where there is a choice, buy the sun-dried varieties (or second best, freeze-dried) rather than those dried by artificial heating. Dried fruits will keep for up to a year or even longer if you choose to deep-freeze them. They are often considerably cheaper if bought in bulk and if you have storage space this is the most economical way to purchase them.

RAW VEGETABLES AND FRUITS

Raw fruits and vegetables contain all their original nutrients and fibre and many studies have been published in recent years which confirm the valuable contribution that salads and fresh fruits make to a healthy diet and the prevention of disease. It is therefore a good idea to eat at least one salad a day and some fresh fruit.

VEGETABLE AND FRUIT JUICES

Raw fruit and vegetable juices provide an excellent way of obtaining the nutrients of fruits and vegetables in a quick, convenient and concentrated form. Juices are rich in vitamins, minerals, enzymes and natural sugars and they are easily assimilated by the blood stream. Carrot and celery juice are good staple ingredients and they are useful for combining with other stronger tasting vegetable juices that do not taste too good on their own. Pineapples, pears and apples serve the same role in the preparation of fruit juices. Among many others the following juice combinations are both nutritious and tasty – carrot and apple; carrot and tomato; carrot and celery; orange and pineapple; papaya and pineapple; orange and grapefruit; carrot, apple and lettuce (in 5:3:1 proportions).

Eggs, Yoghurt and Cheese

EGGS

Eggs contain a lot of high quality protein. They also contain cholesterol and cholesterol-rich diets have been linked to heart disease. However, in small amounts cholesterol is an essential nutrient and in moderation including eggs or egg dishes in your diet is a good idea. Free range eggs taste better and contain none of the chemicals sometimes present in battery hen eggs. They cost more, but, when you can afford them, it is still worthwhile buying them if you can find a reliable supplier.

YOGHURT

Yoghurt is an excellent food. It is nourishing, good for the digestion and a versatile ingredient. Yoghurt also has the reputation of promoting longevity and for being a good stamina food. It may be used in the preparation of soups and salads as a marinating agent, in main meals and in desserts, and even as a summer drink mixed with water, a pinch of salt and mint.

Home-made yoghurt is easy to make and it is much fresher, tastier and more economical than most of the shop-bought varieties. The process simply involves the addition of live yoghurt to a batch of sterilized plain milk maintained at blood temperature – 89°F (37°C). The first source of live yoghurt can be bought at any health or wholefood store, and after that you just reserve some of your home-made yoghurt for use in making your next batch.

Making yoghurt at home possesses some of the mystique attached to breadmaking, but it is basically a simple and foolproof process. Below is given a method that should always work. If you do not have the time or inclination to make it, buy live yoghurt from a health or wholefood store. Some of the thick Greek varieties now on sale are excellent.

Making yoghurt

Put 1–2 pints (500 ml–1 litre) of fresh milk (depending on how much you want to make) in a clean saucepan and bring to the boil. As soon as it bubbles, switch off the heat and transfer the milk to a clean ceramic or glass bowl. Allow the milk to cool to about blood temperature 98–100°F (37–38°C). To test, put your finger into the milk, which should be comfortably warm. If you like, you can use a thermometer, although I never do. Now stir in 1–2 tablespoons (15–30 ml) of live yoghurt, cover the bowl with a lid and wrap the whole thing in a thick towel. Store in a warm place (e.g. the airing cupboard, above the pilot light on a gas stove, above the hot area at the back of the fridge, in the sun or near a radiator; some people pour the cultured milk into a thermos flask). Leave to set for 10–12 hours, when the yoghurt will be ready for use. Store in a refrigerator.

For a thick yoghurt, add 1–2 tablespoons (15–30 ml) of powdered milk to the fresh milk before starting. If you want to make a really large amount of yoghurt, make it in several smaller batches rather than in one huge quantity. For some reason it seems to work better that way.

Your first attempt at yoghurt making may produce quite a thin runny yoghurt. Don't worry – this is quite usual, and it will get thicker the third or fourth time of making as your own culture (live yoghurt 'starter') improves.

Thick yoghurt is a cheap, healthy and simple alternative to whipped cream. It is easily made from your own yoghurt or from shop-bought natural yoghurt. Take a traditional jelly bag and pour in 1 pint (500 ml) natural yoghurt. Hang the bag over a sink or a large bowl and leave to drain overnight. In the morning gently press the yoghurt and turn it into a bowl – it is now ready for use. A sieve lined with damp cheese-cloth can be used instead of a jelly bag.

CHEESE

Cheese, apart from being a delicious food and a versatile ingredient for the cook, is also relatively high in protein and a good source of the mineral calcium and Vitamins A and D. As with other dairy products, it also has a fairly high saturated fat content although cheeses like mozzarella and ricotta contain less than the average cheese. Cheese should therefore be eaten in moderation and, where suitable, low fat varieties used for cooking.

COOKING CHEESES

Cheddar Cheese   This is a traditional English cheese originally from Somerset, but Cheddar-type cheeses are now made all over Britain and imported from other countries. It can be mild or strong in flavour depending on the time it is left to ripen. The texture is smooth and it melts evenly in cooked dishes.

Cottage Cheese   A low fat, soft, granular textured cheese made from skimmed milk, it has a milky flavour and may be used in savoury and sweet dishes.

Emmenthal   A hard, Swiss cheese with irregularly spaced large holes, it has a distinctive flavour. Use as for Gruyère (see page 41).

SATURATED FAT CONTENT OF COMMON CHEESES, MILK AND YOGHURT

	Fat content % of total weight
Camembert	26
Cottage Cheese	4
Cream Cheese	70
Edam	26
English Cheeses (e.g. Cheddar, Cheshire)	33
Feta	25
Gouda	27
Gruyère	32
Mozzarella	19
Ricotta	15
Milk (whole)	3.5
Milk (skimmed)	2
Yoghurt (whole)	3.4
Yoghurt (low fat)	1.5

Gruyère A hard Swiss cheese with regularly spaced, small holes, it has a creamy, slightly acid flavour. It melts smoothly for cooking and sauce making and is best known in fondue dishes.

Mozzarella This is an Italian soft cheese with very little taste of its own, but with excellent melting qualities that make it useful to the cook, especially in pizza making. Originally made only from buffalo milk, the more rubbery cows' milk version is now more common. The best Italian mozzarrella is very white, moist and moderately elastic. It is sold for export in plastic bags containing some liquid to keep the cheese fresh. Once opened, store mozzarella in the refrigerator in a covered container containing a little, lightly salted water.

Ricotta   Made from cows' or sheeps' milk, ricotta is a soft
moist cheese not dissimilar to cottage cheese. It is most useful
in savoury dishes containing cheese fillings, such as ravioli or
filled pancakes, as well as in dessert and cake making. Ricotta is
at its best very fresh and should be bought as needed.

Parmesan   A very hard, strongly flavoured cheese, it is ideal
for grating. Used in cooked dishes and for sprinkling over pasta,
soups and polenta.

Note: Dishes containing cheese should not be overcooked or
overheated. Under such conditions some cheeses, particularly
the hard ones, get rubbery, tough and difficult to digest.

Nuts and Seeds

In general nuts and seeds are delicious and highly nutritious
foods, whether eaten raw on their own or used as part of a
recipe.

To blanch nuts put them in a pan of boiling water and allow
to stand for 2–3 minutes (longer for hazelnuts, cobnuts and
filberts). Drain, rinse in cold water and rub off the skins.

Roasting Nuts and Seeds
Preheat the oven to 325°F (170°C, gas mark 3). Spread the whole
or chopped nuts or seeds on a baking tray and place them in the
oven. Bake them for about 10 minutes giving them a shake once
or twice during this time. The nuts or seeds are ready when
lightly browned.

Nuts and seeds may also be pan roasted on top of the oven.
Put them in an ungreased, heavy frying pan and gently toss
them about over a moderate flame until lightly browned.

THE VEGETARIAN PANTRY

The kitchen is a workplace and as such needs to be clean and clear of unnecessary equipment and unwanted ingredients. It is uneconomic and bad planning to buy fresh foods and to then use old items you have in stock. So throw out items you have been saving 'just in case' and discard any dried goods, such as rice, beans and pasta, that you have had for more than six months. Efficient food preparation even on a budget requires that you have essential ingredients in stock and that they are uncluttered, easy to get at and easy to put away again. Below is a list of suggested pantry cupboard ingredients. Keeping such a selection in stock will make the preparation of many different types of meals and most of the recipes in this book convenient. Those ingredients in italics are highly recommended. Items that are best bought fresh on a weekly basis are included in the weekly store list at the end.

Oils (preferably cold pressed) *olive oil*; a *neutral oil* such as peanut or sunflower; sesame and safflower oil

Herbs (preferably fresh, otherwise dried) *oregano, mint, bay leaves, basil,* thyme, rosemary, sage

Spices (whole seeds preferably) *black pepper, cumin, coriander, cinnamon, turmeric, sea salt,* white pepper, curry powder, cayenne, mustard seeds, caraway seeds, cloves, allspice

Vinegars *organic cider vinegar,* rice wine vinegar, wine vinegar

Flavourings *naturally fermented soya sauce* (shoyu), *hot pepper sauce, fresh ginger root, garlic, vegetable stock cubes, tahini,* peanut butter, creamed coconut, miso, honey

Grains and pulses *long grain brown and white rice, 100 per cent wholemeal flour (stoneground),* 81 per cent wholemeal flour, *strong white flour, bulgar wheat,* couscous, *dried pasta* (including egg noodles), *red and brown lentils, chickpeas and red beans, your own favourite grains and beans*

Canned goods   *plum tomatoes*, chickpeas, red beans, sweetcorn, tomato purée

Bottled goods   olives, mustard, chutney

Nuts and seeds   *sesame seeds*, sunflower seeds, walnuts, almonds

Dried fruits   not essential but useful

Weekly store   *natural yoghurt, lemons, milk, beancurd, cheese, eggs*

BASIC KITCHEN EQUIPMENT

The recipes in this book do not require any special equipment, although an electric blender is recommended. In fact, from the author's experience, a few items of essential, good quality, hand operated equipment (except for blender), together with a sizeable easy-to-clean work surface and the best cookware you can afford are the main priorities of good cooking. Below is a list of the suggested basic pieces of kitchen equipment. I have not recommended cheap items, since in the long term good equipment often turns out to be the best buy and you have the added pleasure of enjoying its quality.

KNIVES AND CHOPPING BOARD

An 8 in (20 cm) to 19 in (25 cm) stainless steel cook's knife and a paring knife are essentials. Stainless steel is harder to sharpen than carbon steel, but it will not blacken or discolour foods such as avocados, red cabbage and fruits as the latter will. Keep your knives sharp by honing them after use on a steel sharpener. For periodic sharpening use an oil stone. Blunt knives are paradoxically more dangerous than sharp ones, since they are more likely to slip off the food being cut and on to your fingers. Sharp knives also require less force to cut with.

A decent sized wooden chopping board is a pleasure to work on. Hardwoods such as maple or sycamore are the longest lasting. A wooden board will protect the cutting edge of the knife and provide a good slip free surface for the food being chopped.

BLENDER

This is essential for some recipes and also for those times when you are in a rush. With one you can make dressings, dips, sauces, purées and soups in minutes or even seconds. The blender should have its own place on the work top in a readily accessible position. This is much more convenient and quicker than if it is put away in a cupboard after each use.

SAUCEPANS AND A WOK

Stainless steel saucepans are the best if you can afford them. They are hardwearing, easy to clean and a pleasure to cook with. Enamelware is almost as good, but if it chips it leaves base metal exposed. Aluminium cookware is to be avoided if possible. It scratches easily and leaves deposits of the metal in the cooking food. It also discolours some vegetables and sauces. Non-stick pans are fine while the coating lasts, but once it starts to wear off they have the same problems as aluminium pans. Perhaps a very good, heavy non-stick frying pan is a worthwhile buy if it is looked after very carefully. This or a heavy stainless steel frying pan may also be used as a substitute for a wok in those recipes where one is recommended. A wok is the curved-bottomed circular pan used in Chinese cooking. It is perfectly designed for quick stir-fried dishes, deep frying, sautéeing and simmering, in fact for all the different methods of cooking done on top of the stove. For use on a conventional hot plate or gas ring, it needs to be supported on a small metal frame, which can usually be purchased with the wok.

OTHER BASIC EQUIPMENT

Garlic press – large ones are easier to use and more efficient.
Lemon or lime juicer – hand held, carved wooden ones are the best and simplest.
Mortar and pestle and/or hand mill – for grinding spices, nuts and seeds.

Pepper mill – black pepper is much better freshly ground and more economical.

Scissors – useful for preparing vegetables and trimming herbs.

Vegetable peeler – swivel bladed ones are the best.

Kitchen scales – the simpler the better. Leave set up ready for use on a worktop.

Wooden spoons

Wire whisk

Colander and sieve

Hand grater

Measuring jug

MENUS

Breakfasts

Main Course

Porridge   *page 62*
Porridge and Plump Fruit   *page 63*
High Energy Oat Cereal   *page 63*
Millet Porridge   *page 64*
Muesli   *page 64*
Nutty Breakfast Crunch   *page 65*
Date and Apricot Medley   *page 65*
Stewed Prunes and Prune Whip   *page 66*
Hot Grapefruit   *page 67*
Fruit Yoghurt   *page 68*
Oatcakes   *page 68* – serve with cheese
Fruit Medley   *page 69*
Apple Purée   *page 69* – serve with Porridge or Muesli

Supplements

Yoghurt (plain)
Brown Toast
Grapefruit
Pure Fruit Juice
Boiled Eggs
Croissant

Lunch

Light

Lentil Lemon Soup   *page 82*
Tahini and Lemon Dip   *page 85*
Fresh Fruit (optional extra)
★
Carrot and Coriander Soup   *page 78*
Apple and Celery Salad with Curry Dressing   *page 110*
Cheese and Biscuits (optional extra)
★
Clear Soup with Lemon and Beancurd   *page 84*
Nutrition-Plus Coleslaw Salad   *page 105*
Cucumber Dip   *page 87* (optional extra)
★
Coriander Mushrooms   *page 90*
Carrot and Apple Salad   *page 103*
Fruit Yoghurt   *page 68* (optional extra)
★
Tofu Dip with Crudités   *page 93*
Peanut Cheeseburgers   *page 131*
★
Hot Potato Salad   *page 109*
Stuffed Tomatoes   *page 117*
★
Spiced Yoghurt and Onion Salad   *page 104*
Spring Rolls   *page 125*
★
Chinese Greens with Peanut Dressing   *page 106*
Rice Croquettes   *page 151*
★
Healthy Waldorf Salad   *page 108*
Baked Potatoes and Cheese   *page 130*
★
Vegetable Salad with Hot Sauce   *page 111*
Cheese Pie in Minutes   *page 143*

Substantial

Spicy Root Vegetable Soup   *page 75*
Aioli with Crudités   *page 92*
Cheese and Bread or Baked Potato and Cheese   *page 130*

★

Noodles and Chinese Cabbage Soup   *page 74*
Brown Rice and Chickpea Salad   *page 100*
Green Salad

★

Cold Cucumber Soup   *page 82*
Greek Feta Salad   page 101
Avocado and Lemon Dip   *page 85*

★

Mushroom Pâté   *page 95*
Tomatoes Baked with Cheese   *page 143*
Fresh Fruit

★

Root Vegetable Cheese Gratin   *page 113*
Boiled Rice *or* Couscous   *page 25*
Green Salad

★

Stir-Fried Vegetables   *page 127*
Plain Buckwheat   *page 159*
Spiced Yoghurt and Onion Salad   *page 104*

★

Thick Oatmeal and Vegetable Soup   *page 78*
Bean and Pasta Salad   *page 102*

★

Aloo Tari   *page 116*
Boiled Rice   *page 25*
Cucumber Dip   *page 87*

★

Kidney Bean and Cider Casserole   *page 177*
Green Salad

★

Simple Fried Rice   *page 153*
Beansprout and Cucumber Salad   *page 105*

Dinner

Light

Fresh Tomato Soup   *page 72*
Cheese Rice Cakes   *page 154*
Simple Cucumber Salad   *page 109*
★

Japanese Clear Soup with Three Garnishings   *page 80*
Tea and Rice   *page 152*
Two–Colour Cabbage and Tangerine Salad   *page 106*
★

Egg and Lemon Soup   *page 76*
Savoury Potato Cakes   *page 121*
Fresh Fruit Compote   *page 218*
★

Coriander Mushrooms   *page 90*
Chilli Hot Stir-Fried Vegetables   *page 128*
Rice Croquettes   *page 151*
★

Radish and Cheese Dip   *page 86*
Watercress and Pear Salad   *page 110*
Oat and Herb Rissoles   *page 164*
★

Beansprout and Cucumber Salad   *page 105*
Cashew and Almond Pilau   *page 158*
Healthy Banana Delight   *page 224*
★

Apple and Celery Salad with Curry Dressing   *page 110*
Stir-Fried Vegetables   *page 127*
Boiled *(page 25)* or Fried Rice   *page 153*
Rose-Flavoured Apples   *page 216*
★

Savoury Potato Cakes   *page 121*
Chatchouka   *page 135*
Green Salad
Rhubarb Pudding   *page 226*
★

Fresh Tomato Soup   *page 72*
Coriander Mushrooms   *page 90*
Courgette Eggah   *page 146*
Nutty Pear Crumble   *page 222*
★

Watercress and Pear Salad   *page 110*
Vegetarian Lasagne with Cheese Topping   *page 170*
Cheese and Biscuits
Fresh Fruit

Substantial

Black-Eyed Bean Soup and Croûtons   *page 71*
Cheese Pie in Minutes   *page 143*
Nutty Pear Crumble   *page 222*
★

Egg and Lemon Soup   *page 76*
Stuffed Courgettes with Apricots   *page 118*
Rose-Flavoured Apples   *page 216*
★

Bamboo Shoots and Greenbean Soup   *page 79*
Japanese Spicy Aubergines   *page 123*
Boiled Rice   *page 25*
Fresh Fruit
★

Cashew Nut and Tofu Pâté   *page 94*
Green Rice   *page 154*
Stir-Fried Vegetables   *page 127*
★

Aubergine and Tahini Dip   *page 86*
Soft Fried Noodles   *page 172*
Baked Apples   *page 219*
★

Vegetable Salad with Hot Sauce   *page 111*
Beancurd and Fried Rice   *page 182*
Banana Fans   *page 216*
★

Aioli with Crudités   *page 92*
Soft Fried Noodles   *page 172*
Green Salad
Apple, Banana and Lemon Dessert   *page 223*
★
Chickpeas Spanish Style   *page 180*
Plain Bulgar Wheat   *page 160*
Beetroot, Apple and Yoghurt Salad   *page 107*
Pashka   *page 222*
★
Bulgar Wheat with Cheese and Aubergines   *page 162*
Greek Feta Salad   *page 101*
Baked Apples   *page 219*
Cheese and Biscuits
★
Chickpea and Vegetable Curry   *page 187*
Spring Rolls   *page 125*
Boiled Rice   *page 25*
Spiced Yoghurt and Onion Salad   *page 104*
Fresh Fruit Compote   *page 218*

Dinner Parties

Light

Chilled Beetroot Soup   *page 83*
Parsnip Mousse with Toasted Almonds   *page 94*
Carrot and Apple Salad   *page 103*
Piperade   *page 134*
Banana Fans   *page 216*
★
Carrot and Coriander Soup   *page 78*
Tofu Dip with Crudités   *page 93*
Apple and Celery Salad with Curry Dressing   *page 110*
Stuffed Courgettes with Apricots   *page 118*
Fresh Fruit Compote   *page 218*
★

Cold Cucumber Soup   *page 82*
Various Mezze   *page 89*
Savoury Potato Cakes   *page 121*
Stir-Fried Vegetables   *page 127*
Tofu Cheesecake   *page 212*
★

Fresh Tomato Soup   *page 72*
Spinach, Mushroom and Croûton Salad   *page 96*
Lettuce Soufflé   *page 147*
Tahini and Lemon Dip   *page 85*
Carrot Cake   *page 213*
★

Japanese Clear Soup with Three Garnishings   *page 80*
Japanese Spicy Aubergines   *page 123*
Green Rice   *page 154*
Two-Colour Cabbage and Tangerine Salad   *page 106*
Fresh Fruit
★

Aubergine and Tahini Dip   *page 86*
Cold Cucumber Soup   *page 82*
Pear and Avocado Salad with Tahini Mayonnaise   *page 90*
Stuffed Tomatoes and Cheese Balls   *page 145*
Semolina Halva   *page 217*

Substantial

Potato and Carrot Soup   *page 75*
Coriander Mushrooms   *page 90*
Spiced Vegetable and Lentil Roast   *page 118*
Nutrition-Plus Coleslaw Salad   *page 105*
Gooseberry Pound Cake   *page 215*
★

Black-Eyed Bean Soup and Croûtons   *page 71*
Aioli with Crudités   *page 92*
Romana Pasta   *page 174*
Fruit and Almond Charlotte   *page 219*
★

Rich Vegetable and Rice Soup   *page 76*
Mushroom Pâté   *page 95*
Kidney Beans and Cider Casserole   *page 177*
Simple Carrot Salad   *page 103*
Apricot Rice Pudding   *page 224*

★

Lentil Lemon Soup   *page 82*
Cashew Nut and Tofu Pâté   *page 94*
Cheese, Pasta and Vegetable Bake   *page 169*
Green Salad
Carob Cake   *page 214*

★

Noodles and Chinese Cabbage Soup   *page 74*
Sweet Smelling Coconut Rice   *page 158*
Thai Curried Beancurd and Vegetables   *page 181*
Banana Fans   *page 216*

★

Vegetable Miso Soup   *page 77*
Green Lentil Wholewheat Lasagne   *page 189*
Healthy Waldorf Salad   *page 108*
Plums in Spiced Custard   *page 220*
Cheese and Biscuits

Afternoon Teas

The following breads, cakes, scones and spreads (with bread) are all suitable for serving with tea for an afternoon break. For a more substantial meal you could add brown toast, sandwiches, cheese, a grain salad and so on.

Yeasted Bread Rolls   *page 201*
Muesli Tea Bread   *page 212*
Slightly Sweet Wholemeal Fruit Bread   *page 206*
Wholemeal Bread   *page 202*
Lyn's Orange and Hazelnut Tea Bread   *page 205*
Date and Oat Slices   *page 209*

Oatmeal Scones   *page 211*
Carrot Cake   *page 213*
Carob Cake   *page 214*

Quick Spreads for Sandwiches

Sweet Peanut Sesame Butter   *page 88*
Avocado and Honey   *page 88*
Tahini and Cumin Spread   *page 88*

Menus for Children and Teenagers

Fresh Tomato Soup   *page 72*
Baked Potato with Cheese   *page 130*
Nutty Pear Crumble   *page 222*
★

Lentil Lemon Soup   *page 82*
Quick Pizza Sandwich   *page 208*
Healthy Banana Delight   *page 224*
★

Tofu Dip with Crudités   *page 93*
Beans and Pasta in Tomato Sauce   *page 171*
Fresh Fruit Compote   *page 218*
★

Radish and Cheese Dip   *page 86*
Lyn's Savoury Slices   *page 209*
Apricot Rice Pudding   *page 224*
★

Sweet Peanut Sesame Butter   *page 88*
and Pancakes   *page 149*
Banana Fans   *page 216*
★

Avocado and Honey Spread (served as a dip)   *page 88*
Buckwheat Omelette   *page 134*
Fruit and Almond Charlotte   *page 219*
★

Cucumber Dip   *page 87*
Chilli Beans   *page 177*
Green Salad
★

Tahini and Lemon Dip   *page 85*
Bean and Pasta Salad   *page 102*
Gingered Carrot Salad   *page 99*
★

Tofu Burgers   *page 182*
Stir-Fried Vegetables   *page 127*
Apricot Fudge   *page 221*
★

Carrot and Apple Salad   *page 103*
Red Rice   *page 155*
Date and Oat Slices   *page 209*
★

Lentil Lemon Soup   *page 82*
Oat and Herb Rissoles   *page 164*
Carob Cake   *page 214*
★

Stuffed Tomatoes   *page 117*
Rice Croquettes   *page 151*
Fresh Fruit

Buffets

Choose a selection from the following suggestions. For more variety or for hot buffet dishes, you could of course add to this list, selecting from the many other recipes in this book.

Cold Soups

Cold Cucumber Soup   *page 82*
Chilled Beetroot Soup   *page 83*
see Soups *(page 70)* for hot soups

Dips

Pâtés

Salads

(see page 97 for many other salads)

Vegetable Dishes

Eggs Yoghurt and Cheese

Peanut Cheeseburgers   *page 131*
Courgette and Tomato Cheese Flan   *page 142*
Courgette Eggah   *page 146*
Watercress and Onion Quiche   *page 141*
Stuffed Tomatoes and Cheeseballs   *page 145*

Grains

Cashew and Almond Pilau   *page 158*
Yellow Rice with Spices   *page 155*
Buckwheat Croquette   *page 159*
Red Rice   *page 155*
Oat and Herb Rissoles   *page 164*
Corn on the Cob   *page 165*
Polenta   *page 163*

Beans

Lentil Cayenne   *page 176*
Virginia Black-eyed Beans   *page 180*
Rich Bean, Vegetable and Chestnut Hotpot   *page 184*
Tofu Burgers   *page 182*
Red Cooked Beancurd and Cucumber   *page 183*

Breads, Savoury Baked Goods and Cakes

Yeasted Bread Rolls   *page 201*
Moroccan Bread   *page 204*
Walnut, Almond and Rice Loaf   *page 207*
Oatmeal Scones   *page 211*
Savoury Oat Slices   *page 210*
Cheese and Oat Fingers   *page 211*
Tofu Cheesecake   *page 212*
Carrot Cake   *page 213*
Carob Cake   *page 214*

Desserts

RECIPES

BREAKFASTS

PORRIDGE

Serves 4

A great deal has been written about the preparation of this apparently simple dish; probably as many different ways of making it have been recommended as there are Scots. One interesting idea is that porridge should be made by gradually adding pinches of uncooked oatmeal to the pot as the porridge boils, so that when the dish is ready it contains a range of textures, from completely cooked to raw oatmeal. This is perhaps a method to experiment with.

There are two main things to remember when making porridge. Firstly, do not add the salt until the oatmeal is well swollen, otherwise the salt hardens the meal and prevents proper swelling. Secondly, use a heavy pot and a long cooking time over a very low heat.

1 pt (575 ml) water	salt to taste
4 oz (100 g) porridge oats	cold cream or milk

Bring the water to the boil in a pot and slowly sprinkle in the oats with one hand whilst stirring briskly with a wooden spoon with the other. Return the pot to the boil, reduce the heat to a very low simmer, cover and cook for 20 minutes. Then season to taste with salt. Cover again and cook for a further 10 minutes. Stir occasionally during cooking. Serve with milk or cream. Traditionally the milk or cream is served in individual bowls and each spoonful of hot porridge is dipped into it before being eaten.

Variations
Serve with honey or sugar and dried or fresh fruit.

PORRIDGE AND PLUMP FRUIT *Serves 3-4*

3 oz (75 g) porridge oats	1¼ pints (900 ml) boiling water
2 oz (50 g) dried fruit such as sultanas and/or chopped apricots	skimmed or semi skimmed milk
	ground cinnamon

Put the oats and dried fruit into a heavy pan. Add the boiling water and stir to mix well. Cook over a low heat, sufficient to maintain a very slow boil, with occasional stirring for 15 minutes. Add more water for a thinner consistency. Serve with milk and a pinch of cinnamon.

Note: If you use quick-cooking porridge oats plump up the fruit (by soaking it in hot water for 10 minutes) before adding it to the cooking pot.

HIGH ENERGY OAT CEREAL

This is a breakfast cereal designed to start the day full of energy. Make more than you need and store the rest in an airtight tin.

1 lb (450 g) quick-cooking porridge oats	4 oz (100 g) sunflower seeds
2 oz (50 g) dried apricots	2 oz (50 g) raisins
2 oz (50 g) dates, chopped	4 oz (100 g) mixed roasted nuts

Combine all the ingredients and serve portions with milk, honey and chopped banana.

MILLET PORRIDGE   *Serves 2*

This is a delicious change from oat porridge.

5 oz (125 g) millet flakes	dates or raisins to garnish
¾ pint (450 ml) water	maple syrup to taste
milk to taste	

Mix the millet flakes with half of the water in a saucepan. Add the rest of the water and cook until the mixture thickens (about 12–15 minutes). Serve with milk and chopped dates or raisins, and add maple syrup for a special sweet treat.

MUESLI   *Serves 1*

Muesli was formulated by Dr Bircher-Benner over 70 years ago. He was a well-known, if slightly off-beat, nutritionist, who founded a famous health clinic in Zurich. His recipe for muesli included a mixture of oats, raw fruits, nuts and milk. Although intended as a quick and nutritious food for any time of day, this combination and its derivatives have since become regarded as a breakfast cereal. The recipe was devised to provide a food that supplied good amounts of protein, vitamins, minerals and roughage without overloading the body with too much rich food. His ideas were well ahead of his time and now many of them are supported by medical opinion. Muesli is considered by most nutritionists to be an excellent food combination.

2-3 level tablespoons (30-45 ml) rolled oats	1 level tablespoon (15 ml) roasted chopped nuts
1 eating apple, grated	milk or cream to taste
1 teaspoon fresh lemon juice	honey or brown sugar to taste
2 level tablespoons (30 ml) natural low fat yoghurt	

Grate the apple just before it is needed and then combine it with the oats, lemon juice and yoghurt. Sprinkle the nuts over the top and add milk and honey to taste.

Variations
1   Use dried fruit, soaked overnight, or another fresh fruit in place of the apple.
2   Soak the oats overnight in milk. Muesli prepared this way is softer in texture and more digestible for some people.

NUTTY BREAKFAST CRUNCH   *Serves 6*

Store unused breakfast crunch in an airtight container. Serve it with a topping of chopped dates, raisins and fresh fruit.

3 oz (75 g) vegetable margarine	2 oz (50 g) chopped hazelnuts
1 teaspoon natural vanilla essence	2 oz (50 g) chopped almonds
	2 oz (50 g) wheatgerm
1 tablespoon (15 ml) malt extract	2 oz (50 g) sunflower seeds
8 oz (225 g) porridge oats	

Preheat the oven to 350°F (180°C, gas mark 4). Combine the margarine, vanilla essence and malt extract in a pan and gently melt the mixture. Mix this and all the other ingredients together. Spread the mixture onto a large baking sheet and bake for about 20 minutes in the preheated oven, stirring every 5 minutes. Remove from the oven and allow to cool.

DATE AND APRICOT MEDLEY   *Serves 4*

This breakfast salad is a tasty winter alternative to cereals and grains. It is full of energy, refreshing and a filling start to the day.

6 oz (175 g) dried apricots	½ pint (275 ml) water

4 fl oz (100 ml) apple juice	2 bananas
4 oz (100 g) fresh dates, halved and stoned	

Soak the apricots in the water for 2 hours. Then place in a pan over a gentle heat and cook for 10 minutes. Place in a serving bowl, pour over the apple juice and allow to cool. Chop the dates and slice the bananas into the bowl and mix well. Chill until required. Serve either on its own or with yoghurt.

STEWED PRUNES AND PRUNE WHIP

Serves 4-6

Stewed prunes are a healthy and enjoyable addition to breakfast cereal foods, and for a light breakfast stewed prunes and natural yoghurt are a good combination. They provide energy, useful amounts of Vitamin A and iron and also have a gentle laxative effect. Here is a recipe for stewing prunes followed by a recipe using stewed prunes to make a prune whip. The latter is good on its own or as a sauce over cold sweets.

STEWED PRUNES

8 oz (225 g) dried prunes, covered with cold water and soaked overnight or for at least 6 hours	2 thin slices of lemon

Put the prunes and the soaking liquid into a pan with the lemon slices and bring to the boil. Reduce heat, cover and simmer for 30 minutes or until the prunes are soft.

Set aside to cool and use as required.

Variation
Replace the lemon slices with a small piece of cinnamon stick. Remove the cinnamon stick after stewing the prunes.

PRUNE WHIP

8 oz (225 g) stewed prunes, stoned	1 tablespoon (15 ml) ground almonds
4 fl oz (100 ml) liquid from stewing prunes	1 teaspoon brown sugar
	10 fl oz (300 ml) milk

Put all the ingredients into a blender and process until well puréed. Serve at room temperature or chilled.

Variation
To make chocolate flavoured prune whip, add 2 teaspoons (10 ml) cocoa or carob powder to the blender.

Note: If you wish to make enough stewed prunes for both breakfast use and for preparing a prune whip, double the quantities in the stewed prune recipe. This will provide about enough stewed prunes for breakfast for four people and for making prune whip for four people.

HOT GRAPEFRUIT   *Serves 1*

A hot but fresh and healthy starter for a cold day.

½ grapefruit
1 teaspoon or more honey or maple syrup

Prepare the grapefruit by running a sharp knife around the edge of the flesh and then along and down the segments. Top the grapefruit with honey or maple syrup and place it under a medium high grill for about 5 minutes. Serve immediately.

FRUIT YOGHURT   *Serves 1*

Of course any fruit available could be mixed with yoghurt for a breakfast dish but the combination of grapes, apples and bananas gives a good short- and long-term supply of energy. Use low fat 'live' yoghurt for healthy digestion.

2 oz (50 g) grapes	5 oz (125 ml) low fat, natural 'live' yoghurt
1 banana, sliced	1 tablespoon (15 ml) wheatgerm
1 apple, chopped	

Mix the fruit with the yoghurt and sprinkle wheatgerm over the top.

OATCAKES   *Makes about 20 cakes*

Homemade oatcakes with cheese or just plain butter make a good start to the day.

8 oz (225 g) medium oatmeal	2 oz (50 g) soft vegetable margarine
1 oz (25 g) wholemeal flour	boiling water to mix
1 teaspoon baking powder	

Preheat oven to 375°F (190°C, gas mark 5). Mix together the oatmeal, flour and baking powder. Rub in the margarine and add just enough boiling water to form a firm dough. Knead the dough well and roll it out to ⅛ in (3 mm) thick. Cut the oatcakes out with a plain 2½ in (6 cm) cutter. Place them on a greased baking tray and bake for 10 minutes in the preheated oven. Remove the trays from the oven, transfer the biscuits to a wire grill and cool a little before use. Store unused oatcakes in an airtight container.

FRUIT MEDLEY

Serves 4

This is a good winter breakfast starter and especially tasty in early spring when the first unforced rhubarb is available.

2 oz (50 g) dried prunes, stoned and chopped	1 teaspoon lemon juice
2 oz (50 g) dried apricots, chopped	1 cooking apple, cored and chopped
1 oz (25 g) sultanas	creamed coconut, flaked, to garnish
1 stick rhubarb, chopped	

Put all the ingredients in a saucepan, except for the coconut. Cover with water and cook for 20 minutes. Serve hot or cold, topped with flakes of creamed coconut.

APPLE PURÉE

Serves 4

Apple purée is refreshing on its own, cold, or as a hot topping over cereal.

1 lb (450 g) dessert apples, cored and chopped	grated rind of 1 lemon
6 oz (175 g) sultanas	½ teaspoon ground cinnamon
	½ pint (275 ml) water

Put all the ingredients into a saucepan, bring to the boil, reduce heat and simmer, covered for 10 minutes. Liquidize the mixture in a blender and serve it hot or cold.

SOUPS

VEGETABLE STOCK
Makes 2 pints (1 litre)

3 lb (1.5 kg) vegetables (for a
    stronger flavoured stock choose
    vegetables with a distinctive
    flavour such as leeks, onions,
    parsnips, carrots and celery)

3 pints (1.5 litres) water

2 bay leaves

chopped parsley or other
    available fresh herbs

salt and freshly ground black
    pepper to taste

Wash and roughly chop the vegetables and put them into a pan
with the other ingredients. Stir well, bring to the boil, reduce
the heat, cover and simmer for 45 minutes. Strain off the stock
and gently press the vegetables to extract as much liquid as
possible. Now discard the vegetables. The stock is ready to use,
chill or freeze. If the stock is stored in the refrigerator, it should
be used in three days.

Variations
1   For a darker coloured stock start the recipe by sautéeing the
    onion and other root vegetables used in 2 tablespoons
    (30 ml) vegetable oil until gently browned. Now add the
    water and other ingredients and proceed as above.
2   For an oriental flavoured stock use soya sauce instead of salt
    and add Chinese or Japanese dried mushrooms to the
    ingredients.

QUICK VEGETABLE STOCK
Makes 2 pints (1 litre)

This quick stock is handy to make if you have a food processor
to speedily chop the vegetables. Combinations of root vegetables other than that given in the recipe may be used.

2½ pints (1.4 litres) water	2 tomatoes
2 medium onions	2 cloves garlic
1 medium potato	chopped parsley or other available fresh herbs
1 medium carrot or parsnip	
1 leek	salt and freshly ground black pepper to taste
2 sticks celery	

Put the water into a large pan and bring to the boil. Meanwhile finely chop the vegetables and garlic by hand or in a food processor. Put them into the pan of boiling water and add the other ingredients. Return to the boil, reduce heat, cover and gently boil for 20-25 minutes. Strain off the stock and gently press the vegetables to extract as much liquid as possible. Discard the vegetables. The stock is ready to use, chill or freeze. If refrigerated use within three days.

BLACK-EYED BEAN SOUP WITH CROÛTONS

Serves 4

This is a simple but very tasty soup and with the addition of croûtons, it makes a hearty beginning to a meal.

1 tablespoon (15 ml) vegetable oil	1 tablespoon (15 ml) fresh mint, chopped
3 cloves garlic, crushed	
8 oz (225 g) black-eyed beans, soaked overnight and drained	salt and black pepper to taste
	croûtons (see below)
1½ pints (900 ml) water or stock	
1 tablespoon (15 ml) fresh parsley, chopped	

Heat the oil in a large heavy saucepan, add the garlic and sauté until golden over a moderate heat. Add the beans and water or stock and bring to the boil. Cover, reduce heat and simmer until the beans are tender (about 45 minutes). Five minutes before the end of the cooking time, stir in the parsley and mint, season to taste with salt and black pepper and adjust the thickness with more water or stock as needed. Serve the soup with the croûtons in a separate bowl.

CROÛTONS

To make croutons you need good, firm bread. A single ⅜ in (1 cm) slice from a 2 lb (1 kg) loaf will make enough croutons for 3–4 persons.

Take a 5 in (12 cm) pan and cover it to the depth of ⅜ in (1 cm) with vegetable oil. Place the pan over medium heat. Meanwhile, remove the crusts from your slices of bread and cut the bread into ⅜ in (1 cm) cubes. When the oil has just begun to haze, test its temperature by dropping in one of the bread cubes. It should turn quite rapidly to a golden brown colour. Rescue the cube from the oil, reduce the heat slightly and drop in enough of the bread cubes to loosely cover the bottom of the pan. When these cubes are nicely browned, lift them out with a slotted spoon and drain them on absorbent kitchen paper. Repeat the process until all the bread is used. These croutons are best eaten fresh, but they will keep for a day or two in an airtight container.

GRILLED CROÛTONS

Take a French loaf and cut it into ⅜ in (1 cm) slices. Spread both sides of these slices with butter or brush them liberally with olive oil. Lightly toast both sides of the bread under the grill. Serve them as they are or spread on one side with thyme-flavoured goat cheese or a mixture of equal quantities of Stilton and soft Camembert or pounded anchovies or anything else of your own creation. Toast lightly and serve.

FRESH TOMATO SOUP   *Serves 4*

Make this soup in the summer months when tomatoes are good, cheap and plentiful and fresh basil and oregano are easily available.

2 tablespoons (30 ml) olive oil

1 medium onion, finely chopped

2 cloves garlic, crushed

2 lb (900 g) ripe tomatoes, chopped

1 tablespoon (15 ml) tomato purée

1 tablespoon (15 ml) fresh basil, chopped (or 1 teaspoon dried basil)

½ tablespoon (7.5 ml) fresh oregano, chopped (or ½ teaspoon dried oregano)

salt and freshly ground black pepper to taste

1 pint (550 ml) vegetable stock (or use vegetable stock cube and water)

Heat the olive oil in a heavy saucepan and sauté the onion and garlic, stirring occasionally until lightly browned. Add the tomatoes, tomato purée, herbs and salt and black pepper to taste. Stir over a moderate heat until the tomatoes are broken up. Stir in the stock and bring to the boil. Reduce heat, cover and simmer for 30 minutes. Towards the end of the cooking period adjust the seasoning to taste.

MULLIGATAWNY SOUP WITH YOGHURT

Serves 4

3 tablespoons (45 ml) vegetable oil

2 large onions, diced

1-2 teaspoons curry powder

1 clove garlic, crushed

1 lb (450 g) courgettes, diced small

12 oz (350 g) tomatoes, diced

1 large potato, peeled and diced small

16 fl oz (450 ml) vegetable stock or water

salt and black pepper to taste

4 oz (100 g) cooked rice or pasta (optional)

2 fl oz (50 ml) natural low fat yoghurt

1 tablespoon (15 ml) chopped parsley to garnish

Heat the oil in a large saucepan, add the onions and sauté for 2 minutes. Add the curry powder, garlic, courgettes, tomatoes, potato and stock. Bring to the boil, then gently simmer, covered, for 15–20 minutes (until the vegetables are soft). Season to taste with salt and black pepper. Purée the soup in a blender, re-heat and stir in rice or pasta if desired. Serve garnished with a swirl of yoghurt and a sprinkling of parsley.

NOODLES AND CHINESE CABBAGE SOUP

Serves 6

This is a vegetable version of a popular Thai soup. This soup can be made with most types of noodles.

6 oz (175 g) dried egg noodles

1 tablespoon (15 ml) vegetable oil

3 cloves garlic, crushed

2 pints (1.1 litres) vegetable stock

8 oz (225 g) Chinese cabbage (or other Chinese greens), thinly sliced

soya sauce to taste

4 oz (100 g) beansprouts

1 tablespoon (15 ml) coriander leaves, chopped

2 oz (50 g) roasted peanuts, coarsely crushed

1-2 fresh or dried red chillies, seeded and finely chopped

½-1 tablespoon (7.5-15 ml) white sugar (optional)

Cook the noodles in plenty of boiling water according to the instructions on the packet or until just tender. Drain them and rinse under cold water until cooled to room temperature. Set them aside. Heat the oil in a large saucepan and sauté the garlic until golden. Add the stock and bring to the boil. Put in the cabbage and simmer for 2 minutes. Add soya sauce to taste. Stir in the beansprouts and noodles and simmer until the noodles are heated through. Pour the soup into a tureen and sprinkle over the coriander leaves, peanuts, chilli peppers and sugar (optional). Serve immediately.

POTATO AND CARROT SOUP   *Serves 4*

1 oz (25 g) butter	1 lb (450 g) potatoes, peeled and diced
8 oz (225 g) onions, thinly sliced	
8 oz (225 g) carrots, thinly sliced	bouquet garni (a few parsley stalks, a bay leaf and a sprig of thyme tied together in a bundle)
1 stick celery, thinly sliced (optional)	
1 small white turnip, thinly sliced (optional)	salt and freshly ground black pepper to taste

Melt the butter in a large pan, add the sliced onions and cook over a low heat, uncovered, until they are quite soft. Add the carrots and, if using them, the turnips and celery. Stir well and cook for a further 1-2 minutes. Add the diced potatoes, stir well in and then add enough water to submerge the vegetables by about ½ in (1 cm). Add the bouquet garni and salt, cover and turn up the heat. Once boiling, reduce the heat to a slow simmer and cook for 20 minutes or until the vegetables are soft. Add black pepper, adjust the seasoning and remove the bouquet garni. Allow the soup to cool slightly before beating it with a wooden spoon or, if you prefer, blending it in a liquidizer. Reheat before serving.

SPICY ROOT VEGETABLE SOUP   *Serves 4*

1 medium onion, peeled and finely chopped	1 tablespoon (15 ml) flour
	1½ pints (750 ml) water
1 tablespoon (15 ml) olive oil	2 small parsnips, peeled and diced
1 clove garlic, crushed	1 medium turnip, peeled and diced
¼ teaspoon chilli powder	1 swede, peeled and diced
¼ teaspoon ground ginger	salt and freshly ground black pepper to taste
¼ teaspoon ground cumin	
¼ teaspoon ground nutmeg	

Fry the onion in the oil in a large pan, together with the garlic, chilli powder, ginger, cumin and nutmeg for 2-3 minutes until the onion is soft. Stir in the flour and cook for a further 30 seconds. Gradually add the water, stirring continuously. Add the root vegetables and salt and black pepper to taste. Cover the pan and simmer for 20 minutes until the vegetables are just tender. Stir the soup with a wooden spoon or, if you prefer, partially or wholly blend it. Reheat before serving.

EGG AND LEMON SOUP   *Serves 6*

This is known as *avgolemono supa* in Greece. It is a nourishing soup traditionally eaten as the first meal after a lent fast. Lemon and egg is quite a common combination in Greek cooking. *Avgolemono supa* is good hot or chilled.

2½ pints (1.5 litres) vegetable stock	2 medium eggs
3 oz (75 g) white rice	4 tablespoons (60 ml) lemon juice
salt and white pepper to taste	

Bring the stock to the boil, add the rice and season with salt and pepper if necessary. Simmer, covered, for 15 minutes. Beat the eggs well in a bowl, beat in the lemon juice and then very gradually beat in a cupful of the stock. Slowly stir this mixture into the soup making sure it stays on a low simmer and does not boil. Do not rush this stage. The eggs will curdle if the soup boils. Adjust the seasoning if necessary and serve immediately or chill and serve.

RICH VEGETABLE AND RICE SOUP   *Serves 4-6*

This is a flavoursome 'sweet sour' soup that is filling and nutritious.

2 tablespoons (30 ml) vegetable oil	1 teaspoon dried basil
1 large onion, chopped	1 bay leaf

1 tablespoon (15 ml) wholemeal flour	1 pint (550 ml) water
1 small carrot, scrubbed and chopped	1 small clove garlic, crushed
	soya sauce and/or salt to taste
1 stick celery, chopped	4 oz (100 g) cooked rice
1 teaspoon honey or brown sugar	2 tablespoons (30 ml) roasted sunflower seeds to garnish
1 tablespoon (15 ml) cider vinegar	
14 oz (400 g) canned tomatoes, chopped (reserve juice)	

Heat the oil in a pan and sauté the onion, basil and bay leaf for 5 minutes. Stir in the flour. Add the carrot, celery, honey or sugar, cider vinegar, tomatoes with their juice and the water. Bring to the boil, reduce the heat, cover and cook for 20 minutes. Liquidize the soup in a blender with the garlic, soya sauce and/or salt. Add the cooked rice. Reheat and serve with a sprinkling of roasted sunflower seeds.

VEGETABLE MISO SOUP *Serves 4*

This is a nourishing soup much recommended by macrobiotics.

2 tablespoons (30 ml) vegetable oil	4 oz (100 g) miso (see page 30)
2 oz (50 g) mushrooms, sliced	2 pints (1 litre) clear vegetable stock or water
4 oz (100 g) daikon or turnip matchsticks	2 tablepoons (30 ml) parsley, chopped or 1 sheet nori seaweed, lightly toasted until crisp, then crumbled
1 small onion, diced	
4 oz (100 g) carrot, peeled and grated	

Heat the oil in a large heavy pan and sauté the mushrooms, daikon, onion and carrot. When the onions are soft add the stock or water and bring to the boil. Cream the miso and stir into the soup. Return to the boil, and serve garnished with parsley or nori.

CARROT AND CORIANDER SOUP *Serves 4*

Fresh green coriander is now available all year round from Indian grocery stores and good greengrocers. It gives this soup a distinctive and excellent flavour. Carrots make a light, slightly sweet soup. Other root vegetables such as parsnips or potatoes may be used in place of, or as well as, carrots.

2 teaspoons vegetable oil	2 tablespoons (30 ml) fresh coriander, finely chopped
1 medium onion, finely chopped	salt and black pepper to taste
1 lb (450 g) carrots, peeled (or just scrubbed for young carrots) and finely chopped	freshly ground coriander seeds to garnish
1½ pints (900 ml) vegetable stock or water	

Heat the oil in a heavy based saucepan and sauté the onion and carrots until softened but not browned. Add the stock or water and bring to the boil, reduce heat, cover and simmer for 20 minutes. Stir in the coriander leaves. Ladle three–quarters of the soup into the liquidizer and gently pulse the machine until the soup is smooth. Return it to the pan, add salt and black pepper to taste and heat through. Serve in a tureen or individual bowls, garnished with a pinch of ground coriander.

THICK OATMEAL AND VEGETABLE SOUP *Serves 6*

Oatmeal may of course be added to any soup or stew to thicken it and add flavour. This recipe is very simple and may be used as a basis for more elaborate soups.

2 tablespoons (30 ml) vegetable oil	3 pints (1.5 litres) stock or water
2 medium onions, diced	4 oz (100 g) oatmeal
2 medium carrots, grated	salt and black pepper to taste

Heat the oil in a heavy saucepan and sauté the onions and carrots until they are soft and the onions are starting to brown. Add the stock or water, sprinkle in the oatmeal, stir well and bring to the boil. Reduce heat, cover and simmer. Cook until the soup is well thickened and the oatmeal is cooked, season to taste with salt and black pepper. Serve.

BAMBOO SHOOTS AND GREEN BEAN SOUP
Serves 4-6

This Indonesian soup is served with boiled rice. Some of the soup stock is used to moisten the rice, the soup vegetables are then spooned over it and the stock is served in a separate bowl.

2 pints (1.1 litres) vegetable stock	1 lb (450 g) green beans, topped, tailed, cut into 2 in (5 cm) lengths
1 medium onion, finely diced	
2 cloves of garlic, crushed	4 oz (100 g) tinned bamboo shoots, sliced
1 in (2.5 cm) piece root ginger, finely chopped	
	1 tablespoon (15 ml) lemon juice
1 lb (450 g) tomatoes	salt and black pepper to taste
2 bay leaves	

Heat the stock in a pan and add the onion, garlic and ginger. Bring to the boil, cover and set to simmer. Scald the tomatoes briefly in boiling water, remove the skin and chop them into quarters. Put the tomatoes into the stock pan, add the bay leaves, stir well and season to taste with salt and pepper. Leave the soup to simmer for another 15 minutes. Add the green beans and bamboo shoots, stir well and return the pan to the boil. Reduce the heat to low and simmer, covered, for 15–20 minutes or until the beans are very tender. Stir in the lemon juice, adjust the seasoning and serve with boiled rice (see above).

Variations
1 You can substitute carrots, potatoes, courgettes, aubergines, cabbage etc. for the green beans and proceed as directed.
2 Replace the bamboo shoots with sliced water chestnuts.

JAPANESE CLEAR SOUP WITH THREE GARNISHINGS

Serves 4-6

This soup is served in individual bowls each containing a few tiny pieces of colourful garnishings. Chopsticks are used to pick out the garnishings, and the soup is then sipped directly from the bowl.

2 pints (1.1 litres) clear vegetable
   stock (or use stock cubes)

---

soya sauce to taste

GARNISHINGS

Select one item from each of the following categories (see recipe):

Solid	*Leafy*	*Vegetable*
cooked noodles	celery leaf	potato (cooked)
diced omelette	parsley	white radish (daikon), grated
diced beancurd	watercress	onion, sliced
peanuts	cucumber	beansprouts
boiled egg, sliced	Chinese leaves	green pepper, thinly sliced
		carrot, thinly sliced
		spring onion, chopped
		mushroom, thinly sliced

Heat the stock until boiling and season to taste with soya sauce. Pour the soup into the serving bowls, one per diner, and add the garnishings. Three items, each different in texture, shape and colour should be used. Make a selection from the items suggested above, for instance, for something solid add a few strands of cooked noodles, for something leafy add some chopped celery leaf and, finally, for the vegetable a thin slice of carrot. Alternatively devise your own ideas for garnishings.

THAI MUSHROOM SOUP
Serves 4

This soup and the cabbage soup variation (see below) are simple Thai peasant dishes. They are quick to make and tasty.

1 tablespoon (15 ml) vegetable oil	4 medium sized mushrooms, wiped and thinly sliced
2 cloves garlic, crushed	2 spring onions, finely chopped
½ teaspoon coriander seeds, ground	1 tablespoon (15 ml) finely chopped coriander leaves
2 teaspoons soya sauce	1 fresh or dried red chilli pepper, seeded and thinly sliced (optional)
¼ teaspoon freshly ground black pepper	
2 pints (1.1 litres) vegetable stock (or stock cube and water)	

Heat the oil in a large saucepan and stir in the garlic, coriander and black pepper. Fry, stirring, until the garlic just turns golden. Add the soya sauce and stock and bring to a low simmer. Simmer for 10 minutes, then add the mushrooms. Simmer for a further 5 minutes and then serve the soup garnished with the chopped spring onions and coriander leaves and, if you like hot food, the sliced chilli pepper.

The mushrooms can be replaced with 4 dried Chinese mushrooms, soaked in hot water for 30 minutes, drained, stems removed and discarded and the caps sliced.

Variation

Follow the mushroom soup recipe but replace the mushrooms with 10 oz (300 g) cabbage or Chinese cabbage, thinly sliced. After adding the cabbage simmer for 6 or 7 minutes or until the cabbage is just tender.

COLD CUCUMBER SOUP   *Serves 4*

3 tablesppons (45 ml) white wine vinegar	16 oz (450 g) Greek yoghurt
1 clove garlic, finely chopped	4 tablespoons (60 ml) finely chopped fresh mint or chives
2 medium cucumbers, peeled	salt and pepper to taste

Put the vinegar in a small bowl and add the garlic. Set aside. Thinly slice off 10 or 12 slices of cucumber, set aside and cover. Grate the rest of the cucumber on the coarse section of the grater. Combine with the yoghurt, herbs and seasoning in a large glass bowl. Chill and if too thick dilute with a little iced water. Stir in the strained vinegar, garnish with the cucumber slices and serve.

LENTIL LEMON SOUP   *Serves 6*

A delicious version of lentil soup, it is served topped with fried garlic and onion and fresh lemon juice.

12 oz (350 g) lentils (red, brown or green), washed	juice of 1 lemon
2½ pints (1.5 litres) water or stock	salt and black pepper to taste
1 medium onion, finely diced	2 tablespoons (30 ml) olive oil
1 medium carrot, sliced	2 cloves garlic, crushed
1 teaspoon ground cumin	1 large onion, thinly sliced
	lemon wedges

Put the lentils in a heavy pot with the water or stock, add the finely diced onion and carrot and bring to the boil. Reduce the heat, cover and simmer for 1 hour or until the lentils are very soft. Blend the mixture or push it through a sieve. Return it to the pot and add cumin, lemon juice and salt and black pepper to taste. Return to a gentle simmer for 15 minutes. Heat the oil in a frying pan and sauté the garlic for a minute or two. Add the sliced onion and fry until it is golden brown. Serve the soup in bowls and top each one with a portion of the browned onions and garlic. Serve a side dish of lemon wedges for extra lemon juice if needed.

Variations
In the Middle East this soup is often served with more oil than used in the above recipe, so provide extra oil to sprinkle over at the table. Melted butter can be used in place of olive oil. For a thicker soup add 4 oz (100 g) of uncooked rice or broken pasta 20 minutes before the end of the cooking time.

CHILLED BEETROOT SOUP (BORSCHT) *Serves 4-6*

Try this soup on a really hot day. It is very refreshing as a starter or on its own. Also serve it as a sauce.

2 tablespoons (30 ml) vegetable oil	1¾ pints (1 litre) water
1 medium onion, chopped	1 clove garlic
2 large raw beetroots, chopped	soya sauce to taste
2-3 sticks celery	2 tablespoons (30 ml) chopped fresh parsley
2 teaspoons fresh mixed herbs, chopped, or 1 teaspoon dried mixed herbs	8 oz (225 g) tomatoes or 1 small can, chopped
1 oz (25 g) wholemeal flour	4 oz (100 g) single cream (optional)

Sauté the onions in the oil in a pan for 5 minutes. Add the flour and stir it in well. Add the celery, beetroot, mixed herbs and water. Stir well and bring to the boil. Reduce heat, cover and simmer for 45 minutes (or 20 minutes in a pressure cooker). Liquidize the contents of the pan in a blender with the garlic, soya sauce, parsley and tomatoes. Pour the soup into a serving bowl and chill for at least 5 hours in the fridge. Serve, if you wish, with a swirl of cream in each bowl.

CLEAR SOUP WITH LEMON
AND BEANCURD   *Serves 4*

This is a simple but tasty and visually attractive soup.

1¾ pints (1 litre) clear soup
    stock (made with stock cubes
    if you wish)

6 oz (175 g) beancurd (see page
    31), cut into ½ in (1.25 cm)
    cubes

1 lemon, thinly sliced

1 small leek or 2 spring onions,
    finely chopped

Bring the stock to the boil and add the beancurd. Reduce the
heat and simmer for a few minutes. Divide the soup and
beancurd between four bowls, taking care not to crush the
beancurd. Decorate each bowl with slices of lemon and the
finely chopped leek or spring onion. Do not crowd the bowls
with ingredients. If you have too much lemon or leek, save it
for future use.

Variation
Replace the lemon slices with 2 teaspoons finely chopped ginger
root.

STARTERS, DIPS AND SPREADS

TAHINI AND LEMON DIP   *Serves 4*

This is a straightforward, quite thin, tahini dip which is also good hot, as a sauce with grains or vegetables.

4 fl oz (100 ml) tahini	salt to taste
1 clove garlic, crushed	parsley, chopped to garnish
2 fl oz (50 ml) water	pinch of cayenne to garnish
juice of 1 lemon	
1½ tablespoon (25 ml) vegetable oil (olive oil is best)	

Blend or thoroughly mix the tahini, garlic, water, lemon juice and oil. Add more water if the dip is too thick. Add salt to taste. Serve garnished with parsley and a sprinkling of cayenne.

AVOCADO AND LEMON DIP   *Serves 4-6*

A Mediterranean recipe that is sharp and appetizing.

2 ripe avocados	salt and black pepper to taste
juice and grated rind of 1 lemon	up to 5 fl oz (150 ml) vegetable oil (olive oil is best)
2 cloves garlic, crushed	

Put the avocado flesh, lemon peel, lemon juice and garlic into a blender (or mix by hand) and make a smooth paste. Leaving the paste in the blender, add salt and black pepper to taste. Now put the blender on the slowest speed and slowly add the oil. Stop when the mixture stops absorbing oil easily or when the taste is to your liking. Serve with fresh crusty bread.

AUBERGINE AND TAHINI DIP   *Serves 4*

Serve garnished with black olives and accompanied by warm pitta bread.

2 small aubergines	2 tablespoons (30 ml) finely chopped fresh parsley
4 fl oz (100 ml) tahini	salt to taste
juice of 1 lemon	
1 clove garlic, crushed	

Lightly oil the aubergines and place them in an oven preheated to 350°F (175°C, gas mark 4) for about 1 hour or until the aubergine interiors are well cooked. Rub or peel the skins off (the easiest way to do this is under a running cold tap). Combine the aubergine flesh with the remaining ingredients and blend into a smooth paste.

BEETROOT DIP   *Serves 4*

8 oz (225 g) plain cottage cheese	5 fl oz (150 ml) natural yoghurt (or soured cream)
1 tablespoon (15 ml) mayonnaise	2 small cooked beetroots, grated

Sieve the cottage cheese into a bowl. Stir in the mayonnaise and yoghurt (or soured cream). Just before serving stir in the beetroot.

RADISH AND CHEESE DIP   *Serves 4*

8 oz (225 g) plain cottage cheese	5 radishes
4 oz (100 g) Cheddar cheese, grated	5 fl oz (150 ml) carton plain yoghurt

Sieve the cottage cheese into a bowl. Stir in 3 oz (75 g) of the Cheddar cheese. Finely chop 4 of the radishes and stir in with the yoghurt. Spoon into a dish. Garnish with the remaining Cheddar cheese and radish, sliced.

CUCUMBER DIP

Serves 4

8 fl oz (225 ml) natural yoghurt

4 in (10 cm) piece of cucumber, finely diced

few sprigs of fresh mint, chopped

Combine all the ingredients and serve.

WALNUT, MUSTARD AND CHEESE DIP

Serves 4

8 fl oz (225 g) Cheddar cheese

salt and freshly ground black pepper to taste

pinch cayenne pepper

2 teaspoons prepared English mustard

2 oz (50 g) chopped walnuts

5 fl oz (150 ml) natural yoghurt

Combine all the ingredients and beat them together. Chill and serve.

PEANUT BUTTER SPREADS

Combined with either yeast extract (e.g. Marmite) or miso (see page 30) or with mashed banana, peanut butter makes a delicious spread. Spread slices of wholemeal bread with one of these combinations and serve open-faced or as a sandwich.

SWEET PEANUT SESAME BUTTER

Serves 4

1 oz (25 g) sesame seeds, dry roasted

4 oz (100 g) peanut butter

1 tablespoon (15 ml) honey

¼ teaspoon salt

Combine the ingredients and mix well.

Note: You can use sunflower seeds instead of sesame seeds, or a mixture of both.

AVOCADO AND HONEY SPREAD *Serves 2*

1 ripe avocado, thinly sliced

honey to taste

Scoop out the avocado flesh and mash it with the honey.

TAHINI AND CUMIN SPREAD

Serves 4

4 oz (100 g) tahini

1 clove garlic, crushed

2 teaspoons lemon juice

½ teaspoon ground cumin

1 tablespoon parsley, finely chopped (optional)

Combine the ingredients and mix well.

SPINACH WITH SESAME SEED AND SOYA DRESSING

Serves 4

1 lb (450 g) spinach

salt

4 tablespoons (60 ml) sesame seeds

1 tablespoon (15 ml) sugar

2 teaspoons shoyu (natural soya sauce)

2 teaspoons water or stock

1 tablespoon (15 ml) rice vinegar or cider vinegar

Wash the spinach leaves well. Bring a large pan of water to the boil. Add the spinach and salt and cook very briefly. As soon as the spinach droops, quickly drain it and rinse under cold water until cooled. Drain it well again and gently squeeze out excess water. Chop the spinach into about 1½ in (4 cm) lengths. Toss the spinach in the dressing and serve in deep individual serving bowls with the spinach resting in the centre of the bowl.

Shake the sesame seeds in a dry pan over a moderate heat until they are toasted golden brown. Crush the seeds into a paste with a pestle and mortar. Combine the paste with the remaining ingredients and mix well to dissolve the sugar.

Note: Tahini or Chinese sesame paste may be used in place of the crushed sesame seeds (although freshly crushed seeds are the best).

VARIOUS MEZZE

Mezze or Middle Eastern hors d'oeuvres are an intrinsic part of the culture of that part of the world. They are served like the Western hors d'oeuvres at the beginning of a meal as appetizers, or alternatively in a larger variety as a meal in itself. *Mezze* also make excellent snacks and accompaniments to drinks. Below is a list of simple *mezze* ideas. All of the items on it may be prepared quickly and a selection of them together will provide an unusual and exciting start to a meal. Serve *mezze* with warmed pitta bread.

Olives, on their own or in salad dressings or spiced with a little cayenne
Nuts, a single variety or mixed, plain or roasted
Slices of onion and tomato, arranged in a circle of alternating rings, garnished with chopped parsley or mint
Wedges of cucumber
Chickpeas, soaked, drained, roasted in the oven and salted
Pickles
French beans, cooked, dressed in oil and lemon juice
Shredded, chopped or sliced raw vegetables
Lemon wedges

Radishes on ice
Tahini seasoned with crushed garlic and lemon juice to taste
Ripe avocado flesh, mixed with finely chopped onion and tomato,
   seasoned with salt and black pepper, dressed with lemon juice
   and served on lettuce leaves.

PEAR AND AVOCADO SALAD
WITH TAHINI MAYONNAISE   *Serves 4*

This is a very elegant looking starter and is quick to prepare.
The sauce is quite addictive and larger quantities can be made
up and stored for a week or so in the fridge to accompany other
dishes or as a dip for raw vegetables.

3 teaspoons tahini paste	1 ripe pear
3 tablespoons (45 ml) mayonnaise	2 limes
1 medium ripe avocado	chicory to garnish

Combine the tahini and mayonnaise and mix well together. Peel
the pear and the avocado. Cut each into halves or quarters
lengthways and remove the core and stone. Now cut these
halves or quarters lengthways into fairly thin slices. Divide these
slices between four plates, making a fan shape of alternate slices
of avocado and pear. At the base of the 'fan', place a tablespoon
(15 ml) of the tahini mayonnaise. Slice one of the limes and
arrange as a garnish with the chicory leaves. Squeeze the juice
of the second lime over the pear and avocado arrangements and
serve.

CORIANDER MUSHROOMS   *Serves 4*

Preferably use small button mushrooms, but failing that larger
ones, halved or quartered, will do fine. In either case they must
be very fresh. To avoid the formation of too much liquid during
the cooking stage, sauté the mushrooms in a smallish frying pan
rather than a saucepan and do not cover them. Olive oil is
essential for this dish.

3 tablespoons (45 ml) olive oil	2 teaspoons lemon juice
1 teaspoon coriander seeds, freshly ground	salt and pepper to taste
1 bay leaf	bay leaves and lemon portions to garnish
9 oz (250 g) white button mushrooms, stems trimmed	

Pour the olive oil into the sauté pan and heat it over a medium flame. Add the ground coriander and the bay leaf to the hot oil. Immediately the bay leaf starts to darken, tip in the mushrooms and then the lemon juice. Season with salt and pepper and cook, stirring frequently, for 3–4 minutes or until the mushrooms have a translucent look about them (achieved when the hot oil has penetrated the centre). Adjust seasoning, place in a serving dish or dishes and allow to cool. Garnish with bay leaves and lemon sections before serving.

FRIED AUBERGINE OR COURGETTE SLICES   *Serves 4*

I have given two recipes here, one for a chilled dish and the other for a hot dish.

CHILLED

2 small aubergines, cut into ⅜ in (1 cm) thick slices, or 4 small courgettes, sliced lengthways	2 cloves garlic, thinly sliced
	2 tablespoons (30 ml) cider vinegar
4 fl oz (100 ml) olive oil	salt to taste

Put the aubergine or courgette slices in a colander and generously salt them. Set aside for 30 minutes. Now wash and drain them and pat them dry. Fry the slices in the oil in a heavy frying pan until they are soft and browned on both sides. Layer the slices in a shallow dish, sprinkling each layer with garlic slices, vinegar and salt to taste. Chill and serve.

HOT

2 small aubergines, cut into ⅜ in (1 cm) thick slices, or 4 small courgettes, sliced lengthways	2 cloves garlic
	salt to taste
2 tablespoons (30 ml) vegetable oil (olive oil if possible)	2 tablespoons (30 ml) cider vinegar

To make this Turkish dish, put the aubergine or courgette slices in a colander and salt them generously. Set aside for 30 minutes. Now wash and rinse them and pat them dry. Heat the oil in a heavy frying pan, add the garlic and sauté lightly. Put in the aubergine or courgette slices and brown them on both sides. Place them in a serving dish, season with salt and sprinkle the vinegar over them. Serve hot.

AIOLI WITH CRUDITÉS   *Serves 4-6*

In this recipe plain, crisp raw vegetables are served with aioli sauce. It is refreshing and simple.

CRUDITÉS

8 sticks of celery, cut in half	6 tomatoes, quartered
6 medium carrots, cut into sticks	2 green peppers, sliced
1 medium cucumber, cut into 3 in (7.5 cm) lengths and quartered	small bunch of radishes, trimmed

AIOLI

6-8 garlic cloves	9 fl oz (250 ml) olive oil
salt	white pepper
1 medium egg yolk, beaten	juice of 2 medium lemons

Prepare the vegetables and arrange them decoratively in a serving bowl. Cover with cling film and chill in the refrigerator for about 1 hour.

To prepare the aioli, put the garlic, egg yolk and a little salt in the blender and, with the machine running, add the oil very slowly to form a thick sauce. Season with salt, pepper and lemon juice. Pour into a large serving bowl or 3–4 small ones, cover with cling film and leave in the refrigerator until needed.

Serve the aioli and vegetables together and allow the diners to help themselves.

Variation
If you wish, you can grate the vegetables coarsely (in this case you might substitute beetroot for radishes) and then arrange them in little piles on individual plates. Place a large spoonful of aioli on each plate.

TOFU DIP WITH CRUDITÉS   *Serves 4-6*

Follow the previous recipe for *Aioli with Crudités* but replace the aioli with a low-fat tofu dip.

TOFU DIP

4 oz (100 g) tofu (beancurd – see page 31), drained

2 cloves garlic

4 shallots

¼ teaspoon ground ginger

2 tablespoons (30 ml) fresh parsley or coriander or other fresh herbs

salt and pepper to taste

Combine all the ingredients in a liquidizer and blend until smooth.

PARSNIP MOUSSE WITH TOASTED ALMONDS
Serves 8

This recipe freezes very well. When cooked, allow it to cool down before freezing. When needed, the mousses should be allowed to thaw and then be reheated gently in a *bain-marie* in the oven. It is most attractively presented in individual moulds, but can also be made in one large one.

1¼ lb (550 g) parsnips, peeled	2 tablespoons (30 ml) dry sherry (optional, for special occasions)
¼ pint (150 ml) milk	
¼ pint (150 ml) cold water	grating of nutmeg
½ teaspoon salt	½ oz (15 g) butter
4 oz (100 g) cream cheese	1 oz (25 g) toasted flaked almonds
3 medium egs	

Preheat oven to 375°F (190°C, gas mark 5). Chop the parsnips roughly and bring carefully to the boil with the milk, water and the salt. Simmer carefully until just cooked. Remove from the heat and purée until very smooth. Then beat in the cream cheese, eggs, sherry (if used) and nutmeg (this is all done very easily with a liquidizer). Take 8 individual ramekins and rub the insides with the butter. Divide the almonds among the bases. Alternatively prepare a 1 pint (550 ml) pudding basin and line its base with the almonds. Spoon in the parsnip mixture. Place in the oven in a *bain-marie* and cook until set. Allow to cool for 5 minutes before turning out of the moulds.

CASHEW NUT AND TOFU PÂTÉ
Serves 4-6

This pâté needs almost no cooking. For special occasions use the wine as suggested. Serve with brown melba toast. Roasted, ground nuts other than cashew nuts may be used. Walnuts, peanuts, hazelnuts are all suitable.

1 tablespoon (15 ml) olive oil	4 tablespoons (60 ml) white wine, or water
1 small onion, diced	2 tablespoons (30 ml) chopped parsley
1 small clove garlic, crushed	
4 oz (100 g) cashew nuts, toasted and ground	salt to taste
6 oz (175 g) tofu (beancurd – see page 31), drained	

Heat the oil in a shallow pan and sauté the onion and garlic until softened (about 5 minutes). Add this mixture to the nuts in a mixing bowl, then mash in the tofu. Blend in the wine, parsley and salt. Press the paté into individual ramekins, smooth the top of the mixture and serve.

MUSHROOM PÂTÉ   *Serves 4*

This is a vegetarian pâté served in the same way as a meat paté. It is usually enjoyed by non-vegetarians, since it looks and tastes quite meaty.

12 oz (375 g) mushrooms, washed and chopped	1 small clove garlic, crushed
2 tablespoons (30 ml) vegetable oil	3 tablespoons (45 ml) wholemeal flour
1 large onion, peeled and chopped	1 teaspoon miso (see page 30)
2 tablespoons fresh rosemary or 1 teaspoon dried rosemary	soya sauce to taste

Heat the oil in a pan and sauté the onions, garlic and rosemary for about 5 minutes. Add the mushrooms and cook over a moderate heat for a further 5 minutes. Add the flour and cook with stirring for a further 7–8 minutes. Put the mixture into a blender and add the miso and soya sauce to taste. Beat to a smooth paste. Serve the paté smoothed down in individual ramekins.

STUFFED CELERY AND DATES   *Serves 4*

The stuffing in this recipe can be either a nut and cheese mixture
or a low fat nut and tofu mixture.

4 oz (100 g) cream cheese or tofu (beancurd – see page 31), mashed	4 sticks celery, cut into 2 in (5 cm) lengths
4 oz (100 g) ground hazelnuts or almonds	12 fresh dates, halved and pitted

Combine the ground nuts and cream cheese or mashed tofu and
fill the celery pieces and date halves with the mixture. Arrange
the stuffed celery and dates on four individual white plates and
serve.

SPINACH, MUSHROOM AND CROÛTON SALAD   *Serves 4*

This is a first course salad of dark green spinach leaves with
white crunchy mushrooms and croûtons.

8 oz (225 g) fresh spinach	juice of 1 lemon
8 oz (225 g) small mushrooms	4 tablespoons (60 ml) olive oil
24 CROÛTONS (see page 72)	1 tablespoon (15 ml) white wine vinegar
salt and black pepper to taste	

Wash the spinach and drain it well. Tear the leaves into large
pieces, discarding the stalks. Pile the spinach into a serving
bowl. Wipe the mushrooms, slice them and then squeeze the
lemon juice over them. Put salt and pepper into a small bowl,
add the olive oil and wine vinegar and whisk until blended.
Scatter the mushrooms and croûtons over the spinach, pour the
oil and vinegar dressing over, toss thoroughly and serve.

SALADS

THREE BEAN SALAD

Serves 4-6

This robust salad will keep you well fuelled on a winter's day. The cooked beans are mixed with lots of fresh parsley and it makes all the difference to the flavour of the finished salad.

4 oz (100 g) red beans	½ medium onion, finely chopped
4 oz (100 g) haricot beans	1 clove garlic, crushed
4 oz (100 g) chickpeas	1 tablespoon (15 ml) wine or cider vinegar
4 parsley stalks + 2 tablespoons (30 ml) finely chopped parsley	2 tablespoons (30 ml) olive oil (or other vegetable oil)
1 bay leaf	½ teaspoon cumin seeds, ground
2 sprigs of fresh thyme or 1 teaspoon dried thyme	salt and black pepper to taste

Combine the beans, cover with water and soak overnight. Drain the beans and rinse them. Put them in a saucepan and cover with unsalted water. Bring beans rapidly to the boil, boil for 5 minutes and then reduce to a simmer. Add the parsley stalks, bay leaf and thyme. Cover and cook until all the beans are tender (about 1-1½ hours). Drain the beans (reserve the liquid for later use as stock) and discard the spent herbs. Put the hot beans in a mixing bowl and add the remaining ingredients. Mix well and leave to cool. Adjust seasoning if necessary, before serving.

Variation
Use left–over cooked beans or separately cooked beans to make the salad. Tinned beans can also be used for speed. In this case use only tinned chickpeas and tinned red beans.

INDIAN TOMATO SALAD
Serves 4

This spicy, mint flavoured tomato salad is usually served with curry dishes.

450 g (1 lb) firm tomatoes, quartered	½ teaspoon ground cumin
1 small onion, finely diced	2 tablespoons (30 ml) finely chopped mint
175 ml (6 fl oz) natural yoghurt	salt and black pepper to taste
pinch cayenne	

Combine the tomatoes and onion in a serving bowl. Stir together the yoghurt, cayenne, cumin, mint and salt and black pepper to taste. Gently toss the tomato and onion in this dressing and serve.

COURGETTES WITH PARSLEY SALAD
Serves 4

This is a very simple but effective courgette salad. The recipe calls for dill seeds but you could use the dill seed heads retrieved from a jar of dill pickles. Incidentally, Eastern European countries have a great tradition of pickling and preserving and their products are both very good and reasonably priced.

2 tablespoons (30 ml) vegetable oil	3 tablespoons (45 ml) fresh parsley, coarsely chopped
1½ lb (700 g) small courgettes, thickly sliced	1 teaspoon dill seeds (optional)
4 tablespoons (60 ml) BASIC VINAIGRETTE DRESSING (see page 195)	salt and black pepper to taste

Heat the oil in a pan, add the sliced courgettes and cook over a moderate heat, stirring occasionally for 5–8 minutes. The courgettes should be barely tender and still firm to the bite. Transfer to a colander and chill them completely under cold running water. Place them in a serving bowl. Add the remaining ingredients, toss well together and serve.

WATERCRESS AND RADISH SALAD

Serves 4

Rather delicate looking, this is nevertheless a strongly flavoured salad. Use the freshest watercress and the crunchiest radishes you can buy.

1 bunch watercress, stems trimmed, washed and drained

1 bunch radish, trimmed, washed, drained and chilled for 1 hour or more

½ small head of lettuce, washed and drained (use hearts of Webb's lettuce or small cos lettuce)

BASIC VINAIGRETTE DRESSING (see page 195)

Make a bed of lettuce leaves in rosette fashion in a serving bowl and sprinkle over a little dressing. Thinly slice the radishes and combine them with the watercress. Add vinaigrette dressing to taste and toss the mixture in it. Arrange the dressed radish and watercress on the lettuce leaves and serve.

GINGERED CARROT SALAD

Serves 4

Grated carrot is such a good foil for so many flavours. Here is another simple salad with an exotic touch.

1 lb (450 g) carrots, finely grated

1 walnut sized piece of fresh ginger

1 small clove garlic, crushed

4 tablespoons (60 ml) lemon juice

salt and black pepper

Place the grated carrot in a fair-sized mixing bowl and grate the fresh ginger evenly across the surface. Beat the crushed garlic and the lemon juice together in a cup and then distribute that over the carrot. Season the ingredients with salt and pepper before gently mixing them together. Test seasoning and turn the salad onto a serving dish.

HOT CHICKPEA SALAD   *Serves 4*

The least refined version of this I had served to me from a great
pot in a Moroccan street market – a steaming ladle of chickpeas,
a pointed finger and a nod in the direction of a thick potage of
crushed garlic and olive oil, another nod in the direction of a
bowl containing a mixture of ground dried red chillies and salt.
It is a primitive, powerful and tasty dish, the essence of which
is the rich vapour of olive oil rising from the hot chickpeas.

9 oz (250 g) chickpeas, cleaned and soaked overnight	2 cloves garlic
small onion or shallot	4½ fl oz (120 ml) olive oil
small carrot	2 red chillies, diced
bay leaf and sprig of thyme	1 tablespoon (15 ml salt

Drain the chickpeas and put them and the onion, carrot, bay leaf
and sprig of thyme into a small saucepan. Cover with unsalted
water or, if possible, the liquid residue from cooked spinach.
Bring the contents of the saucepan to the boil, cover and simmer
slowly for an hour and a half or until the chickpeas are tender.

Set the table up with one small bowl containing the cloves of
garlic, crushed and steeped in the olive oil and another bowl
containing the salt ground together with the diced red chillies.
Some people may also want vinegar and some chopped onion
to hand. Spoon the hot drained chickpeas into four small bowls
and serve, each person spooning over the garlic and oil and/or
salt and chilli dressing as desired.

BROWN RICE AND CHICKPEA SALAD   *Serves 4*

Apart from being good sources of vitamins and minerals, brown
rice and beans are complementary protein partners and weight-
for-weight this salad has the same amount of usable protein as
a piece of steak. Do not, however, think it will be heavy and

boring. The finished salad looks moist, colourful and tempting and tastes good.

8 oz (225 g) tinned or cooked and drained chickpeas (or red beans or haricot beans)	1 tablespoon (15 ml) lemon juice
10 oz (275 g) cooked, rinsed and cooled brown rice	2 tablespoons (30 ml) finely chopped parsley
2 tablespoons (30 ml) olive oil	salt and black pepper to taste
1 tablespoon (15 ml) cider vinegar	1 medium carrot, peeled, cut into matchsticks
2 cloves garlic, crushed	1 green pepper, seeded, diced
	1 stick celery, finely chopped

Combine the chickpeas, rice, oil, vinegar, garlic, lemon juice, parsley, salt and black pepper and gently mix well together. Set the mixture aside in the refrigerator to chill for 30 minutes and to give the beans and rice time to absorb the dressing. Now toss in the carrot, pepper and celery and serve.

GREEK FETA SALAD   *Serves 4*

1 small lettuce, leaves torn into bite-size pieces	1 tablespoon (15 ml) finely diced onion
4 oz (100 g) feta cheese, cut into small pieces	½ cucumber, sliced
2 oz (50 g) black olives	3 tablespoons (45 ml) olive oil
2 firm tomatoes, chopped	juice of 1 lemon
	salt and pepper to taste

Put the torn lettuce leaves into a serving bowl. Add the cheese, olives, tomato, onion and cucumber, pour over the olive oil and lemon juice and season to taste with salt and black pepper. Toss well and serve.

HARICOT BEAN AND SWEET SOUR BEETROOT SALAD *Serves 4*

Any type of cooked bean may be used to make this salad, but white beans contrast well with the red beetroot. This is a filling and tasty winter salad good with a main meal, but also fine as a light lunch with bread and cheese.

2 medium cooked beetroot, medium diced	8 oz (225 g) cooked or tinned haricot beans, drained
1 tablespoon (15 ml) butter	salt to taste
2 teaspoons cider vinegar	2 tablespoons (30 ml) soured cream (or plain yoghurt)
2 teaspoons honey	

Put the beetroot in a pan with the butter and gently heat to melt the butter. Stir and add the vinegar and honey. Continue heating to melt the honey and coat the beetroot in the sauce. Pour this mixture over the beans, stir well, salt to taste. Serve dressed in soured cream (or yoghurt).

BEAN AND PASTA SALAD *Serves 4*

This is an excellent hearty winter salad. It has that protein-rich combination of pulse and grain. Here this combination also provides an interesting contrast in textures.

6 oz (175 g) small elbow or shell pasta	4 tablespoons (60 ml) BASIC VINAIGRETTE DRESSING (see page 195)
12 oz (350 g) cooked or tinned chickpeas or red beans, drained	2 tablespoons (30 ml) chopped parsley, preferably the flat continental variety
1 tablespoon (15 ml) olive oil	
1 clove garlic, crushed	2 tablespoons (30 ml) ground roast cumin seed
1 teaspoon prepared mustard	salt and black pepper to taste

Cook the pasta in salted water until it is *al dente* and pour into a colander. Rinse under plenty of cold water and drain. Gently toss the pasta to shake any water out of its cavities. Combine the beans, pasta and olive oil in a small bowl and mix well. Stir in the remaining ingredients and check seasoning before serving the salad at room temperature.

CARROT AND APPLE SALAD *Serves 4*

juice of 1 lemon	salt and black pepper to taste
2 tablespoons (30 ml) vegetable oil (sesame seed or peanut oil are best)	8 oz (225 g) carrots, peeled and grated
	8 oz (225 g) eating apples, grated

Combine the lemon juice and oil and season it with salt and black pepper to make the dressing. Combine the carrot and apple, toss the mixture in the dressing and serve at once.

SIMPLE CARROT SALAD *Serves 4*

This most simple of salads is at its best made with the sweet young English carrots available in late June, early July.

1 lb (450 g) young carrots, scrubbed, finely grated	1 tablespoon (15 ml) lemon juice
2 tablespoons (30 ml) olive oil	salt to taste

Combine all the ingredients. Toss well and serve.

Variation
Add a handful of chopped fresh parsley, fresh fennel or fresh chervil.

SALAD OF GARDEN TRIMMINGS   *Serves 4*

This is a salad for the person with a kitchen garden. It is delicate and best served alone, as a first course or after the main dish.

4 handfuls of mixed young green leaves (lettuce, summer spinach, sorrel, rocket, dandelion, mustard etc.)	1 pinch sugar
	1 tablespoon (15 ml) lemon juice
	3 tablespoons (45 ml) sunflower seed oil
freshly ground black pepper	

Wash the leaves and shake them dry in a cloth. Try not to bruise them. Pile them into a salad bowl. In another bowl, put the pepper and sugar, add the lemon juice and oil and whisk. Pour this dressing over the salad and toss gently. Serve immediately.

SPICED YOGHURT AND ONION SALAD   *Serves 4*

This very simple refreshing salad comes from Sri Lanka. It is an excellent accompaniment to all those robust dishes, such as hearty vegetable casseroles or bakes.

10 fl oz (300 ml) natural yoghurt	a good pinch Madras curry powder
1 tablespoon (15 ml) vegetable oil	salt to taste
1 teaspoon black mustard seeds	2 medium onions, finely sliced

Pour the yoghurt into a mixing bowl. Pour the oil into a small pan and heat it over a medium flame. Add the mustard seeds to the oil and watch closely. Remove the pan from the heat immediately the seeds start splitting. Add the seeds to the yoghurt together with the curry powder and the salt and beat well. Stir in the finely sliced onions, check seasoning and serve.

NUTRITION-PLUS COLESLAW SALAD
Serves 4

Cabbage is available most of the year at low cost and it combines well with many other ingredients to give a wide range of salads. In this recipe cheese and sunflower seeds are added to the cabbage to give a nutritious rich salad.

12 oz (350 g) white or red cabbage, shredded	juice of 1 lemon
1 medium eating apple, grated	2 fl oz (50 ml) vegetable oil
4 oz (100 g) Cheddar cheese, diced small	2 tablespoons (30 ml) wine or cider vinegar
4 oz (100 g) sunflower seeds, dry roasted	salt and black pepper to taste

Combine the cabbage, apple, cheese and sunflower seeds in a serving bowl and mix well together. Beat together the lemon juice, oil, vinegar and salt and pepper to taste. Toss the salad in the dressing and serve.

Variations
Replace the cheese and/or sunflower seeds with one or two of the following: grated carrot; diced green or red pepper; sultanas or raisins; chopped almonds, walnuts or other nuts; caraway seeds; roasted peanuts; cooked, drained lentils or beans; fresh orange slices or pineapple chunks.

BEANSPROUT AND CUCUMBER SALAD
Serves 4

This is a very simple but effective Indonesian salad. It contains no fat but the dressing is quite sweet. Replace the sugar with clear honey if you prefer its flavour. For a more robust dish, toss the finished salad with a handful of roasted, unsalted peanuts.

8 oz (225 g) beansprouts, washed and drained	2 tablespoons (30 ml) finely diced spring onions
1½ medium cucumbers, sliced in half lengthwise, seeded and cut into matchsticks	3 fl oz (75 ml) cider vinegar
	1 tablespoon (15 ml) white sugar
	½ teaspoon salt

Combine the beansprouts, cucumber and onion. Stir the vinegar, sugar and salt together until the sugar dissolves. Toss the salad in this dressing and serve.

TWO-COLOUR CABBAGE AND TANGERINE SALAD
Serves 4-6

Colourful, tasty and with contrasting textures, the tangerines give this Japanese winter salad a Christmas look.

4 oz (100 g) finely shredded white cabbage	2 tablespoons (30 ml) olive or sesame oil
4 oz (100 g) finely shredded red cabbage	1 tablespoon (15 ml) lemon juice
	½ teaspoon salt
2-3 tangerines, peeled and sliced	6 radishes, trimmed, chopped

Combine the shredded cabbage and tangerine slices and mix well together. In a small bowl, stir together the oil, lemon juice and salt and pour the mixture over the salad. Toss the salad gently and then garnish it with the chopped radishes. Serve at once, or cover and refrigerate until needed.

CHINESE GREENS WITH PEANUT DRESSING
Serves 4

This salad is very good with Chinese flowering cabbage (*choi-sum*). This is a green, leafy vegetable with a mild flavour and it ıs most popular with the Chinese. It is available at most Chinese grocery stores all year round. If *choi-sum* is unavailable, the same dressing is good with Chinese white cabbage (*baak-choi*).

8 oz (225 g) Chinese greens (*choi-sum*), washed, trimmed if necessary, tied into bundles	2 tablespoons (30 ml) creamy peanut butter
salt	1 tablespoon (15 ml) soya sauce

Drop the bundles of greens into a pan of lightly salted, slowly boiling water for 2 minutes. Drain the greens, separate them from the bundles and immediately rinse them under cold water until cooled.

Chop the greens into 1 in (2.5 cm) lengths. Mix together the peanut butter and soya sauce (add a little oil if the mixture is too thick). Toss the greens in this dressing and serve them in individual deep serving bowls.

BEETROOT, APPLE AND YOGHURT SALAD   *Serves 4*

I particularly like beetroot so I enjoy this salad a lot. It is especially good in early to mid–summer, when beetroots are small and sweet.

1 lb (450 g) cooked beetroot, diced	2 teaspoons horseradish sauce
1 eating apple, cored and grated	¼ pint (150 ml) natural yoghurt
1 small onion (red skinned preferably), finely sliced	1 tablespoon (15 ml) chopped chives or spring onions to garnish
juice of ½ lemon	

Combine the beetroot, apple, onion and lemon juice. Stir the horseradish sauce into the yoghurt and then pour it over the salad. Mix well and chill before serving. Serve garnished with chopped chives or spring onion.

BANANA, BAMBOO SHOOT AND TOMATO SALAD

Serves 4

Bamboo shoots make a versatile and convenient salad ingredient. They can add crunch and variety to an otherwise ordinary dish. Here bamboo shoots are combined with two ingredients normally conveniently at hand to produce an unusual and delicious salad.

1 banana, peeled and sliced	3 tablespoons (45 ml) vegetable oil
4 medium tomatoes, sliced	¼ teaspoon curry powder
4 oz (100 g) tin bamboo shoots, drained and sliced	salt to taste
juice of 1 lemon	freshly ground black pepper to garnish

Sprinkle the sliced banana with a little of the lemon juice. In a large salad bowl or individual dishes, carefully arrange the banana, tomato and bamboo shoot slices in colourful layers. Whisk together the remaining lemon juice, oil, curry powder and salt to taste and pour this dressing over the salad. Grind over a little black pepper and serve.

HEALTHY WALDORF SALAD

Serves 4

3 red dessert apples, quartered, cored and sliced	2 oz (50 g) sultanas
3 stalks celery, washed and thickly sliced	4 fl oz (100 ml) low-fat yoghurt
	1 teaspoon lemon juice
4 oz (100 g) unsalted peanuts	1 tablespoon (15 ml) chopped parsley
2 oz (50 g) whole hazelnuts	

In a large bowl combine the apples, celery, peanuts, hazelnuts and sultanas. Stir in the yoghurt mixed with the lemon juice. Sprinkle the parsley over and serve.

SIMPLE CUCUMBER SALAD   *Serves 4*

This refreshing and soothing salad is good with spicy hot dishes.

1 medium sized cucumber	3 tablespoons (45 ml) vegetable oil or olive oil
salt and freshly ground black pepper to taste	4 tablespoons (60 ml) plain yoghurt
1 tablespoon (15 ml) wine vinegar	2 tablespoons (20 ml) chopped chives or parsley
1 tablespoon (15 ml) caster sugar	

Slice the cucumber. Place in a colander and sprinkle over a teaspoon of salt. Leave for an hour to allow excess water to be drawn out. Rinse the cucumber under cold water, then dry well. Arrange in a serving dish. Put salt and black pepper to taste into a bowl, add the sugar and vinegar and mix well to dissolve the seasonings. Whisk in the oil, then the yoghurt and most of the chives or parsley. Pour or spoon this dressing over the cucumber. Sprinkle the remaining chopped chives or parsley over the top and serve.

HOT POTATO SALAD   *Serves 4*

1½ lb (700 g) new potatoes	1 tablespoon (15 ml) wine vinegar
2 tablespoons (30 ml) finely chopped onion	salt and black pepper to taste
3 tablespoons (45 ml) olive oil	4 tbsp (60 ml) chopped fresh chives

Cook the potatoes in their skins, drain, peel and cut them into thick slices. Pour over the oil and vinegar and mix very lightly. Add plenty of salt and black pepper and stir in the chopped onions and three-quarters of the chopped chives. Turn the salad into a clean dish and scatter the remaining chives over the top.

APPLE AND CELERY SALAD WITH CURRY DRESSING   *Serves 4*

8 oz (225 g) eating apples, cored and chopped	½-¾ teaspoon curry powder
4 oz (100 g) celery, thinly sliced	3 tablespoons (45 ml) natural yoghurt
2 tablespoons (30 ml) lemon juice	salt and black pepper to taste
3 tablespoons (45 ml) vegetable oil	

Combine the apple and celery in a serving bowl. Stir together the lemon juice, oil, curry powder and yoghurt. Add salt and black pepper to taste and pour this dressing over the apple and celery mixture

Variation
Another good combination with this dressing is carrot and courgettes. Replace the apple and celery by 8 oz (225 g) carrots, coarsely grated, and 8 oz (225 g) young courgettes, finely sliced.

WATERCRESS AND PEAR SALAD   *Serves 4*

Pears go well with peppery flavours and watercress is no exception. Take great care when buying watercress that it is absolutely fresh and that none of the lower leaves are yellow.

½ bunch watercress, washed, drained	1 head of chicory, leaves separated and washed
1 medium ripe pear, quartered and cut across into ¾ in (0.5 cm) slices	2 teaspoons olive oil
	black pepper to taste

Combine the watercress, pear and chicory leaves in a mixing bowl. Pour in the oil and grind in about 4 twists of black pepper from the mill. Toss the salad until pear juice begins to run. Present the salad on individual side plates.

VEGETABLE SALAD WITH HOT SAUCE

Serves 4 or more

For this South-East Asian salad, suitably cut fresh vegetables are dipped into a hot sauce and then eaten in the manner of French crudités. Select a variety of vegetables from those suggested below, remembering to combine a variety of textures, colours and flavours. Present them arranged on a large serving dish around a bowl of the hot sauce.

VEGETABLES

celery, cut into sticks	green peppers, seeded, cut into strips
cucumber, sliced	
watercress, in sprigs	young green beans, left whole
red radishes, whole	chicory leaves
Chinese cabbage, coarsely chopped into strips	green apples, sliced and sprinkled with lemon juice
carrots, cut into sticks	aubergines or courgette slices, browned in a little oil

Prepare all the vegetables and chill while you prepare the sauce.

SAUCE

2 tablespoons (30 ml) soya sauce	juice of 2 lemons
1 tablespoon (15 ml) finely chopped onion	1 tablespoon (15 ml) sugar
	chilli sauce to taste
3 cloves garlic	

Put all the ingredients into a blender and blend to a smooth sauce. Pour the sauce into a serving bowl and serve as described above.

CELERY AND BANANA SALAD AND SPICY DRESSING

Serves 4

½ head celery, washed, cut into
⅜ in (1 cm) sections

3-4 firm bananas, peeled and cut
into ⅜ in (1 cm) rounds

2 tablespoons (30 ml) cumin
seeds

1 teaspoon coriander seeds

1 teaspoon cardamom seeds

7 fl oz (200 ml) natural yoghurt

salt and cayenne pepper to taste

Place the celery and the banana into a mixing bowl. Lightly toast the cumin and coriander seeds in a heavy metal pan until they begin to hop. Empty the seeds into a mortar, add the cardamom and grind lightly. Remove the cardamom husks before adding the spices to the yoghurt in a small bowl. Season the yoghurt with the salt and cayenne pepper and stir well. Add the spiced yoghurt to the celery and banana and fold gently together. Turn into a serving bowl and serve.

VEGETABLE DISHES

ROOT VEGETABLE CHEESE GRATIN

Serves 6

This is a very economical but surprisingly tasty dish.

1 oz (25 g) butter or margarine

2 medium onions, sliced

8 oz (225 g) turnips, peeled, thinly sliced

8 oz (225 g) parsnips, peeled, thinly sliced

1 lb (450 g) carrots, peeled, thinly sliced

2 cloves garlic, crushed

3 tablespoons (45 ml) finely chopped fresh parsley

¾ pint (450 ml) vegetable stock or semi-skimmed milk

1 tablespoon (15 ml) coarse mustard

salt and black pepper to taste

4 oz (100 g) Cheddar cheese, grated

Preheat the oven to 350°F (180°C, gas mark 4). In an oven and flameproof dish (with a lid available), sauté the onion in the butter or margarine until softened. Add the turnips, parsnips and carrots, stir well and sauté for a further minute. Add the garlic, parsley, stock or milk and mustard and bring to a slow boil. Season to taste with salt and black pepper. Cover and bake in the preheated oven for 1 hour or until the vegetables are just tender. Sprinkle over the cheese, switch up the oven to 425°F (220°C, gas mark 7) and bake uncovered for a further 25 minutes.

COURGETTE AND OATMEAL SAVOURY

Serves 5

This makes a good winter supper dish. Other vegetables such as celery or leeks can be substituted for the courgettes.

2 large onions, chopped	4 tomatoes
1 tablespoon (15 ml) vegetable oil	1 lb (450 g) courgettes, coarsely grated
3 oz (75 g) medium oatmeal	4 medium eggs
salt and black pepper to taste	3 oz (75 g) grated Cheddar cheese
½ pint (275 ml) vegetable stock (made with 1 vegetable stock cube)	

Preheat oven to 375°F (190°C, gas mark 5). Fry the onions in the oil until golden in colour. Add the oatmeal and continue cooking for 2-3 minutes. Add seasoning and stock, stirring all the time. Continue cooking for 10 minutes until the mixture thickens. Meanwhile, peel and slice the tomatoes and place them with the courgettes in an ovenproof dish. Beat the eggs and add to the oatmeal mixture, then stir in most of the cheese and pour this sauce over the vegetables. Top with the remaining cheese. Bake in the preheated oven for 45 minutes, checking that the centre is cooked through with a fork before serving.

SWEETCORN PIE

Serves 4

This is a quick and handy way of using left-over mashed potatoes.

8 oz (225 g) grated cheese	1 lb (450 g) mashed potato
1 small onion, grated	salt, black pepper and nutmeg to taste
1 lb (450 g) tomatoes, skinned and chopped	

11½ oz (315 g) tin of sweetcorn, drained

½ teaspoon dried basil

large knob of low-fat margarine

Preheat the oven to 400°F (200°C, gas mark 6). Add the cheese, onion and tomatoes to the mashed potato. Mix well, season to taste with salt, black pepper and nutmeg. Spread half of the mixture in a shallow buttered casserole, smoothing down well to form the base of the pie. Spread the sweetcorn over this potato base and sprinkle the basil over it. Spread with the rest of the potato mixture to cover. Rough–up with a fork and dot with margarine. Bake for 30–40 minutes in the preheated oven, until golden brown.

NORMANDY MUSHROOM LAYER
Serves 4

3 small onions, sliced

4 large tomatoes, sliced

8 oz (225 g) mushrooms, sliced

8 oz (225 g) Brie, thinly sliced

1½ lbs (675 g) potatoes, peeled and sliced thinly

salt and black pepper to taste

½ teaspoon dried marjoram

5 fl oz (150 ml) thick natural yoghurt

Preheat the oven to 400°F (200°C, gas mark 6). Layer the first 5 ingredients in a casserole dish. Sprinkle each layer with marjoram and season to taste. Finish with a layer of potatoes and pour the yoghurt over the top. Cover and bake for 45 minutes. Serve with a green salad.

CAULIFLOWER CURRY   *Serves 4*

Cauliflowers are delicious cut into florets, dipped into batter and then deep fried, or eaten raw added to salads or as part of a selection of crudités. Cauliflowers are also delicious in curries, especially when the florets are not overcooked, providing extra texture and flavour in contrast to the other well-cooked vegetables, as in this dish.

3 tablespoons (45 ml) olive oil or other vegetable oil	2 tablespoons (30 ml) plain flour
1 medium onion, finely chopped	1 pint (550 ml) vegetable stock
1 medium aubergine, cut into ½ in (1 cm) cubes, salted, pressed and rinsed	salt and freshly ground black pepper to taste
	1 small cauliflower, cut into florets
2-3 teaspoons mild curry powder or paste	2 oz (50 g) seedless raisins
12 oz (350 g) tomatoes, quartered	1 tablespoon (15 ml) chopped fresh coriander

Pour the oil into a saucepan, heat and sauté the onion and aubergine with the curry powder for 2–3 minutes, stirring all the time. Add the tomatoes and sauté for a further 1 minute. Stir in the flour, stock and salt and black pepper to taste. Cover and simmer for 8–10 minutes or until the aubergine is nearly tender. Add the cauliflower and raisins and cook a further 5–8 minutes or until the cauliflower is just tender but still with some crunch. Serve on a bed of white or brown rice, garnished with the chopped coriander.

ALOO TARI   *Serves 4*

Aloo is the Indian word for potato. There are many *aloo* dishes in Indian cuisine, some familiar in the West because of their popularity in Indian restaurants. *Aloo gobi* (potato and cauliflower) and *aloo samosa* are two such dishes. The recipe given here is for a potato curry. It can be served as part of a meal or on its own with natural yoghurt, chutney, chapatis and/or rice.

2 tablespoons (30 ml) vegetable oil	½ teaspoon cayenne pepper
1 lb (450 g) potatoes, peeled and diced	1 teaspoon salt
	2 medium tomatoes, chopped
1 teaspoon turmeric	14 fl oz (400 ml) hot water
1 teaspoon cumin seeds	natural yoghurt
½ teaspoon coriander seeds, crushed or coriander powder	

Gently heat the oil in a heavy saucepan. Add the spices and salt and stir and simmer for 2 minutes. Add the potatoes and stir well so they are well coated with the spice–oil mixture. Simmer for a further 5 minutes. Add the tomatoes and cook for 2–3 minutes. Pour in the hot water, bring to the boil, reduce the heat and simmer, uncovered for 20 minutes or until the potatoes are tender. Serve either with the yoghurt contained in a separate bowl for addition according to taste, or pour 4 fl oz (100 ml) of yoghurt into the curry, stir, heat through and serve.

STUFFED TOMATOES   *Serves 4*

4 beefsteak tomatoes	3 oz (75 g) grated cheese
2 oz (50 g) wholemeal breadcrumbs	1 clove garlic, crushed
1 medium onion, chopped	a pinch of dried chives
1½ oz (40 g) low-fat margarine	

Preheat oven to 400°F (200°C, gas mark 6). Wash the tomatoes, remove and reserve a slice from each top and scoop out the pulp. Chop this finely and leave on one side. Place the tomato cases, side by side, in a greased baking dish. Fry the onion in ½ oz (15 g) margarine until golden brown. Add the chopped tomato pulp and all the other ingredients. Fill the tomato cases with this mixture and replace the tops. Dot with remaining margarine and bake in the preheated oven for 10–15 minutes. Serve.

STUFFED COURGETTES WITH APRICOTS

Serves 4

This is a delicious combination of rice, vegetables and fruit.

4 medium courgettes, sliced lengthways

3 tablespoons (45 ml) olive oil

1 medium onion, diced

8 oz (225 g) long grain rice

8 fl oz (225 ml) water

1 tablespoon (15 ml) tomato purée

½ teaspoon (2.5 ml) sugar

1 teaspoon (5 ml) ground cinnamon

salt and black pepper to taste

16 fl oz (450 ml) water

1 tablespoon (15 ml) honey

8 oz (225 g) dried apricots, diced

juice of 1 lemon

Scoop the pulp out of the courgettes, leaving shells about ¾ in (2 cm) thick. Chop up the scooped-out pulp. Heat the oil in a heavy pan, add the onion and courgette pulp, and sauté until the onion is just soft. Add the rice, 8 fl oz (225 ml) water, tomato purée, sugar, cinnamon and salt and black pepper to taste. Bring to the boil, reduce to simmer, and cook for 15 minutes with occasional stirring. Meanwhile cover the courgette shells in boiling salted water and leave for 2-3 minutes. Drain them, stuff them with the rice mixture, and set aside. Combine the 16 fl oz (450 ml) water, honey and apricots and boil until the apricots are completely softened. Preheat the oven to 350°F (175°C, gas mark 4). Spoon into a heavy casserole dish half the apricots and their juice, place the stuffed courgettes on top, and pour over the remaining apricots and juice. Sprinkle with the lemon juice and bake for 30 minutes or until the courgettes are just soft and tender. Serve hot or cold.

SPICED VEGETABLE AND LENTIL ROAST

Serves 4

Couscous gives this savoury dish a lovely light texture, but if you do not have it, you can use flour, breadcrumbs or any other grain to give more body.

5 oz (150 g) red lentils, washed	¾ teaspoon ground turmeric
1 medium onion, chopped	sea salt to taste
1 medium carrot, scrubbed and chopped	1 oz (25 g) couscous
	½ teaspoon yeast extract
1 stick celery, scrubbed and chopped	2 oz (50 g) wholemeal breadcrumbs
½ teaspoon ground cumin	1 oz (25 g) vegetable margarine
½ teaspoon ground coriander	

Put the lentils, onion, carrot, celery, cumin, coriander, turmeric and salt in a saucepan. Just cover with water, bring to the boil, cover and simmer for 30 minutes, stirring occasionally. Sprinkle in the couscous and cook for a further 5 minutes. Preheat the oven to 400°F (200°C, gas mark 6). Transfer the contents of the pan to an ovenproof dish and spread the yeast extract over the mixture. Cover with breadcrumbs and dot with margarine. Bake for 30–45 minutes in the preheated oven.

NUT ROAST WITH TOMATO AND BASIL SAUCE
Serves 4

Make the sauce for this dish whilst the nut roast is cooking.

1 oz (25 g) margarine	4 oz (100 g) unsalted peanuts
6 oz (175 g) onion, finely chopped	6 oz (175 g) fresh brown breadcrumbs
3 oz (75 g) Brazil nuts, finely chopped	1 tablespoon (15 ml) soya flour
	1 tablespoon (15 ml) arrowroot
3 oz (75 g) hazelnuts, finely chopped	salt and black pepper

Preheat the oven to 350°F (180°C, gas mark 4). Melt the margarine in a large saucepan and sauté the onion in it until golden brown. Mix in the nuts, breadcrumbs, soya flour and arrowroot and season well with salt and pepper. Oil a 1½–2 lb

(700–900 g) loaf tin. Press the nut mixture evenly into the tin. Bake in the preheated oven for about 45 minutes or until golden brown. Cool the roast for a few minutes before turning it out of the tin. Pour the tomato and basil sauce (see below) over the roast and serve.

SAUCE

8 large ripe tomatoes, skinned	pinch of sugar
1 small onion, finely chopped	½ teaspoon dried basil
1 tablespoon (15 ml) vegetable oil	salt and black pepper to taste

Cut the tomatoes into quarters and remove the seeds. Chop the flesh roughly. Sauté the onion in the vegetable oil until soft and transparent. Add the chopped tomato, the pinch of sugar and the basil. Cook over a low heat until most of the liquid has evaporated. Season to taste with salt and black pepper.

SWEET AND SOUR RED CABBAGE WITH CHESTNUTS
Serves 4

This dish is good on its own and also ideal for spicing up a bland savoury dish.

1 medium onion, chopped	2 teaspoons soya sauce
1 tablespoon (15 ml) vegetable oil	1 teaspoon cider vinegar
½ medium cooking apple, chopped	10 fl oz (275 ml) water
1 small red cabbage, thinly sliced	1 teaspoon arrowroot pasted with 1 tablespoon (15 ml) water
1 oz (25 g) sultanas	
2 teaspoons lemon juice	4 oz (100 g) tinned chestnuts, rinsed and drained
1 tablespoon (15 ml) brown sugar	

Sauté the onion in the oil in a pan for 5 minutes. Add the apple and cook for 1 minute. Add the red cabbage, sultanas, lemon juice, brown sugar, soya sauce and cider vinegar. Stir well and pour the water in. Bring to the boil, cover, reduce the heat and simmer for about 15 minutes. Stir in the chestnuts, then the arrowroot paste to thicken. Cook and stir for another few minutes and serve.

JERUSALEM ARTICHOKES, GREENS AND GARLIC
Serves 4 (as side dish)

Make good use of Jerusalem artichokes while they are in season. They are a lovely vegetable and a nice change from potatoes.

3 cloves garlic, crushed	4 oz (100 g) greens (broccoli, kale, spinach etc) or sprout tops, chopped
2 tablespoons (30 ml) vegetable oil	
8 oz (225 g) Jerusalem artichokes, scrubbed, knobs cut off, sliced	soya sauce to taste

Sauté the garlic in the vegetable oil in a pan for 1 minute. Add the Jerusalem artichokes and cook stirring for about 7 minutes over a moderate heat, adding a little water if necessary to prevent browning. Add the greens and cook for a further 5 minutes. Season to taste with soya sauce and serve immediately.

SAVOURY POTATO CAKES
Serves 4

These are good with a salad in the summer, with lightly boiled or steamed vegetables in colder months, or as a snack.

8 oz (225 g) raw potato, grated	2 teaspoons dried sage
2 medium onions, grated	salt to taste
4 oz (100 g) plain flour	oil for shallow frying

Combine all the ingredients together in a bowl and mix well. Form the mixture into 12 small, hamburger-shaped potato cakes. Heat the oil in a frying pan and fry the cakes for about 5 minutes, turning them once during this time. Serve immediately.

INDIAN VEGETABLE KICHIRI   *Serves 4*

The English breakfast dish kedgeree was derived from this Indian recipe in which lentils, brown rice and vegetables are cooked together in one pot.

2 tablespoons (30 ml) vegetable oil	1 teaspoon powdered cinnamon
1 medium onion, thinly sliced	½ teaspoon ground turmeric
1 medium carrot, grated	¼ teaspoon ground cloves
8 oz (225 g) long grain brown rice, washed, drained	1½ pint (850 ml) water, boiling
	salt to taste
4 oz (100 g) green or brown lentils, soaked overnight, drained	1 banana, sliced
2 tablespoons (30 ml) dessicated coconut, lightly dry roasted	2 oz (50 g) roasted almonds or peanuts
1 teaspoon cumin seeds	

Heat the oil in a large pan and sauté the onions until just soft, add the carrots and continue sautéing until the onions are coloured light brown. Put in the rice and lentils and fry over a low heat, stirring, for 5 minutes. Add the coconut and spices, mix well and cook, stirring for a further 2 minutes. Pour in the water, mix, season to taste with salt. Reduce the heat to as low as possible, cover the pan and simmer for 45–50 minutes or until all the liquid is absorbed and the rice and lentils are tender. Serve garnished with the slices of banana and roasted almonds or peanuts.

JAPANESE SPICY AUBERGINES

Serves 4 (as a side dish)

1 lb (450 g) aubergines cut into ¾ in (2 cm) cubes, salted, pressed, rinsed and drained

4 tablespoons (60 ml) vegetable oil

2 teaspoons finely grated root ginger

1 clove garlic, crushed

1 medium onion, finely sliced

pinch cayenne pepper or Japanese seven spices pepper

3 fl oz (75 ml) vegetable stock or water

1 teaspoon sugar

1 tablespoon (15 ml) finely chopped chives or parsley or 1 sheet nori seaweed, toasted and crumbled

Heat the oil in a heavy pan, add the aubergines and sauté for 3–4 minutes. Stir frequently. Remove the aubergines from the pan, drain and reserve the oil. Put the aubergines to one side and return the drained oil to the pan. Add the ginger, garlic, onion and cayenne and sauté over a high flame for 30 seconds. Reduce the heat, pour in the stock and sugar and mix well. Add the aubergines and bring to the boil. Turn off the heat and serve garnished with chives or parsley or nori.

NEW POTATOES WITH SPINACH IN YOGHURT DRESSING

Serves 4

Potatoes and spinach make splendid bedfellows. The stringent slightly bitter taste of the spinach gives the rather dour-tasting potatoes a necessary lift. If you have bought spinach for another meal select the smaller, fresher leaves for this dish. Use slightly larger new potatoes rather than the very small ones.

1½ lb (700 g) new potatoes

2 oz (50 g) spinach leaves, shredded

½ bunch spring onions, chopped

juice of ½ lemon

5 oz (150 ml) natural yoghurt

salt and freshly ground black pepper to taste

Wash the potatoes clean under a running tap. Do not scrub or peel them, just cut out any damaged areas. Drop them into a pan of boiling salted water and cook on medium heat for 20 minutes or more. Sometimes new potatoes are very dense and take a surprisingly long time to cook. Test by lifting one of the larger ones out with a wooden spoon and giving it a gentle squeeze. If it gives a little it's cooked. Drain potatoes and set aside in a serving bowl to cool. Set aside a small amount of shredded spinach leaves and spring onions for later garnishing and then combine the remaining ingredients with the potatoes in the serving bowl. Mix well, garnish with reserved spinach and spring onions and serve.

COS LETTUCE IN
CREAMY SAUCE   *Serves 2-4*

Cream sauces in Chinese cooking are fairly rare. This Chinese dish has a delicate flavour.

1 good head cos lettuce	½ oz (15 g) cornflour
4 fl oz (100 ml) milk	2 oz (50 g) peanut oil
salt to taste	½ teaspoon sugar
4 fl oz (100 ml) vegetable stock	1 tablespoon (15 ml) butter

Cut out and discard the lettuce core. Separate the lettuce leaves. Leave the small leaves whole and chop the larger ones into 4 in (8 cm) lengths. Rinse and drain well, then pat dry. Combine the milk, salt and vegetable stock and set aside. Put the cornflour into a bowl and add about 3 tablespoons (45 ml) of the milk and stock mixture and set aside. In a wok or frying pan heat 3 tablespoons (45 ml) of the oil and when it is hot turn off the heat. Add the lettuce and then turn the heat to high, cooking, turning and stirring the lettuce for about 1 minute. Add the sugar and salt to taste. Cook for about 3 minutes then quickly transfer the lettuce to a serving dish with a slotted spoon. Wipe out the pan. Heat the remainder of the oil in the pan and add the milk and stock mixture and the cornflour mixture. Bring to the boil stirring constantly. When thickened, turn off the heat and stir in the butter. Add more salt if necessary. Spoon the sauce over the lettuce and serve immediately.

SPRING ROLLS

Serves 6

This recipe has been slightly Westernised to suit the availability of particular ingredients, but the spring rolls are nevertheless delicious and very popular with almost everybody.

The pancakes for making spring rolls are quite easy to make but you can, if you wish, buy them pre-made in any relatively well-stocked Chinese grocery store.

Spring rolls skins, as they are known to the Chinese, are thin and made from an egg-rich batter.

BATTER

5 oz (150 g) plain flour, sifted

1 oz (25 g) cornflour

4 eggs

15 fl oz (450 ml) water

or 12 pre-made spring roll skins

vegetable oil for shallow and deep frying

FILLING

1 tablespoon (15 ml) vegetable oil

1 green pepper, seeded, thinly sliced

2 sticks celery, finely chopped or 4 oz (100 g) bamboo shoots, finely chopped

2 spring onions, finely chopped

1 clove garlic, crushed

1 teaspoon peeled, grated ginger root

6 oz (175 g) mushrooms, sliced

12 oz (350 g) beansprouts, washed and drained

2 tablespoons (30 ml) fish sauce or soya sauce

2 fl oz (50 ml) water

GARNISH

finely chopped mint leaves

Combine the batter ingredients, except the oil, in a mixing bowl or electric blender and beat into a smooth batter. Brush the bottom of a 8 in (20 cm) frying pan with a thin coating of the oil and heat it over a medium flame. Pour in enough batter to very thinly cover the bottom of the pan. As soon as the bottom side starts to brown turn the pancake over and just cook the other side. Remove the pancake from the pan and repeat the procedure until almost all the batter is used up (about 12 pancakes). Reserve a little of the batter (about 2 tablespoons (30 ml) for sealing the spring rolls (see below). Stack the cooked pancakes one on top of the other.

Heat 1 tablespoon (15 ml) oil in a large frying pan or wok and over a medium flame stir-fry the green pepper and celery for 2 minutes. Add the spring onions, garlic and ginger and stir-fry for another 1 minute. Add the mushrooms and beansprouts and stir-fry for a further minute. Add the fish or soya sauce and water and continue stir-frying until the beansprouts are well wilted. Remove the pan from the heat.

Divide the filling between the cooked pancakes (or pre-made spring roll skins). Spoon the filling onto each one and roll it up, tucking in the edges as you go. Seal the flap with a little of the reserved batter thickened with a little flour.

Deep-fry the filled spring rolls in deep, hot vegetable oil (peanut oil is traditionally used) until crisp and golden brown. Drain and serve immediately, garnished with mint leaves.

ODEN   *Serves 6-8*

A popular Japanese winter casserole, oden is often prepared for festive occasions when people help themselves out of the oden pot, which can bubble away all evening without spoiling. In some big cities, vendors sell oden in the streets. From experience I can tell you they are not keen on customers who want to pick and choose from the oden pot. They believe in pot luck.

2 pints (1.1 litres) stock	1 tablespoon (15 ml) soya sauce
1 tablespoon (15 ml) sugar	2 medium carrots, cut into 2 in (5 cm) pieces

8 oz (225 g) baby turnips or daikon, chopped	4 oz (100 g) cabbage, coarsely chopped
8 oz (225 g) new potatoes, scrubbed	salt to taste
12 oz (350 g) pressed beancurd, cut into 2 in (5 cm) pieces	

Bring the stock to the boil in a large pot and add the sugar and soya sauce. Add the carrots, turnips or daikon and potatoes and simmer, covered, for 15 minutes. Add the beancurd, cabbage and salt. Simmer, covered, for another 15 minutes or until all the vegetables are tender. Transfer the oden to a warmed tureen and serve.

STIR-FRIED VEGETABLES *Serves 4*

Stir-frying is an excellent method of cooking vegetables. They are cooked so quickly in their own juices that very little of their nutritional content is lost. The important thing to remember is to have all the ingredients chopped and ready before you start cooking. Once the stir-fry is ready, it should be served at once. The following is a sample recipe; you may wish to use a different selection of vegetables.

4 tablespoons (60 ml) vegetable oil	6 oz (175 g) leeks, carefully cleaned, finely chopped
2 tablespoons (30 ml) peeled and grated fresh ginger root	6 oz (175 g) cauliflower florets
6 oz (175 g) Chinese leaves, shredded	soya sauce to taste
6 oz (175 g) Brussels sprouts, finely chopped	freshly ground black pepper to taste (optional)

Heat the oil in a wok or deep frying pan and sauté the ginger for less than a minute. Add the prepared vegetables and stir-fry for 4–5 minutes. The vegetables should remain slightly crunchy. Add the soya sauce to taste while continuing to stir the vegetables. Add black pepper to taste. Serve immediately.

CHILLI HOT STIR-FRIED VEGETABLES

Serves 4

This South-East Asian recipe can be used for one or a combination of vegetables. If using more than one vegetable, add those vegetables that take the longest to cook to the pan first.

1 lb (450 g) total weight washed and chopped vegetables (select one or more from French or green beans, stringed, chopped; carrots, sliced; celery, chopped; beansprouts; cabbage, shredded; green or red peppers, seeded, cored, sliced; courgettes, sliced)

2 tablespoons (30 ml) vegetable oil

1 clove garlic, crushed

1 small onion, finely sliced

1 or 2 dried chillies, seeds removed, chopped

2 bay leaves

1 teaspoon grated lemon peel or 1 stalk lemon grass, chopped

2 teaspoons dark soya sauce

salt to taste

Heat the oil in a wok or deep frying pan and add the garlic, onion, chilli, bay leaves and lemon peel or lemon grass. Stir-fry the mixture until the onion is softened. Add the vegetable or mixed vegetables (in the correct order, the hardest first) and stir-fry until they are all lightly cooked but still crunchy. Add soya sauce and then, if necessary, salt to taste. Stir well and serve immediately.

BRUSSELS SPROUTS AND CHESTNUTS WITH CARROT AND CHEESE SAUCE

Serves 4-6

Brussels sprouts, stir-fried in olive oil, with onion rings, broccoli florets, strips of red pepper and a pinch of cayenne makes a delicious, spicy dish, which is quick and easy to prepare. Or try them in this more substantial dish.

1 lb (450 g) Brussels sprouts	¾ pint (450 ml) skimmed milk
½ medium cauliflower, divided into florets	3 oz (75 g) grated cheese
	½ teaspoon dried mustard
1 small can of whole, peeled chestnuts, rinsed and drained	salt and freshly ground black pepper to taste
1 oz (25 g) vegetable margarine or butter	3 medium carrots, peeled and grated
1 oz (25 g) plain flour	

Preheat oven to 180°C (350°F, gas mark 4). Cook the sprouts and cauliflower in separate pans of boiling salted water until just tender but still crisp. Do not use too much water. Drain the vegetables. Refresh under cold water and drain again. Arrange the vegetables and the chestnuts in a greased ovenproof dish. Melt the margarine or butter in a saucepan. Stir in the flour and cook for 30 seconds. Gradually add the milk, stirring continuously. Add the cheese, mustard, salt and black pepper, continually stirring until the cheese is melted. Finally add the carrot and pour the sauce over the vegetables and chestnuts. Cook in the preheated oven for 15 minutes until the top is golden brown.

Note: This dish can be assembled up to 8 hours in advance. Cover and keep in the refrigerator. Cook as above before serving.

BAKED POTATOES
AND CHEESE
Serves 4

4 large potatoes, washed

8 oz (225 g) cottage cheese

salt (optional)

Preheat oven to 400°F (200°C, gas mark 6). Cut a wide cross on each potato. Sprinkle some salt, if desired, over each. Wrap in foil and bake for one hour or until tender. Press the base of the potatoes to open the crosses, then pile some cottage cheese onto each. Serve immediately.

EGGS, YOGHURT AND CHEESE

QUICK FRIED CABBAGE WITH EGGS
Serves 2

This is a Chinese variation on scrambled eggs.

1 tablespoon (15 ml) vegetable oil	salt and pepper to taste
1 medium onion, finely sliced	pinch of chilli powder
8 oz (225 g) cabbage or Chinese cabbage, finely shredded	2 eggs, beaten

Heat the oil in a heavy frying pan or wok and fry the onion in it until softened. Add the cabbage, salt and pepper and a pinch of chilli powder. Stir-fry for 2–3 minutes and then cover the pan and cook the mixture over a low heat for 10 minutes. Now stir in the beaten eggs and scramble them with the cabbage. As soon as the egg has set, serve.

PEANUT CHEESEBURGERS
Makes 4 large burgers

Serve as a healthy tasty alternative to a Big Mac.

1 tablespoon (15 ml) vegetable oil	2 oz (50 g) wholemeal breadcrumbs
½ medium onion, finely diced	4 oz (100 g) cheese, grated
2 oz (50 g) mushrooms, sliced	salt and black pepper to taste
4 oz (100 g) crunchy peanut butter	1 egg, beaten
2 oz (50 g) sesame seeds, lightly dry roasted	wholemeal flour for coating
2 tablespoons (30 ml) tahini	oil for shallow frying
juice of 1 lemon	

Heat the vegetable oil and sauté the onion until softened. Add the mushrooms and sauté for a further minute. Combine this mixture in a bowl with the peanuts, sesame seeds, tahini, lemon juice, breadcrumbs, cheese and salt and pepper to taste. Stir well and mix thoroughly. Press the mixture into four burgers, brush them with the beaten egg and then coat them with a light sprinkling of wholemeal flour. Shallow fry until nicely brown on both sides and serve.

CORIANDER CREAM EGGS AND MUSHROOMS
Serves 4

This is a colourful, cold salad dish of boiled eggs and mushrooms in a delicious coriander cream sauce.

4 fresh eggs	juice of ½ lemon
5 fl oz (150 ml) coriander cream sauce (see below)	about 20 black olives
4 oz (100 g) white mushrooms, stalks trimmed off	4 sprigs of coriander to garnish

Hard-boil the eggs. Cool them under running water, shell and quarter them. Take four, plain, white, side plates. Place a good heaped tablespoon of the coriander cream sauce in the centre of each. Arrange the quartered eggs (4 quarters per plate), yellow side up, around this. Finely slice the mushrooms and arrange them around the eggs. Sprinkle lemon juice over the mushrooms. Scatter the black olives over the plates and garnish the completed salad with the coriander sprigs.

CORIANDER CREAM SAUCE
This soft mellow sauce is good with eggs, pasta, salads and white fish.

½ bunch fresh coriander	1 tablespoon (15 ml) lemon juice
2½ oz (75 ml) single cream	½ tablespoon (7.5 ml) French mustard
2 tablespoons (30 ml) neutral oil (eg, sunflower or peanut)	salt and black pepper to taste

Wash the coriander well and shake it dry. Cut away all but the finest stems. Place the trimmed leaves in a liquidizer or food processor. Add the rest of the ingredients and blend well together at medium speed until a smooth green sauce is obtained. Test the seasoning before using.

SPINACH AND YOGHURT CRÊPES
Serves 4

These are good on their own or with a cheese or tomato sauce (see pages 197 and 199).

4 oz (100 g) wholemeal flour	1½ lb (800 g) fresh spinach, finely chopped
1 egg, beaten	4 tablespoons (60 ml) natural yoghurt
10 fl oz (275 ml) milk	
2 tablespoons (30 ml) vegetable oil	nutmeg
1 tablespoon (15 ml) vegetable margarine	salt and pepper

Place the flour in a large mixing bowl, make a well in the centre of the flour and add the egg. Gradually whisk in half the milk and beat until smooth. Add the remaining milk and 1 tablespoon (15 ml) of oil.

Heat a 6 in (15 cm) omelette pan and wipe round the inside with a piece of absorbent paper dipped in a little of the remaining oil. Pour in enough batter to coat the base of the pan thinly. Cook until the underside is brown, turn over and cook for another 10–15 seconds. Turn out onto greaseproof paper. Repeat with the remaining batter, making 12 pancakes in all. Stack with greaseproof paper between them, to prevent them sticking. Melt the margarine in a saucepan over a low heat. Add the spinach and cook for 5 minutes, stirring occasionally. Remove from the heat and stir in the yoghurt, then season with nutmeg, salt and pepper. Place a portion of the filling in the centre of each pancake, roll up like a cigar and place under a hot grill to warm through. Serve immediately.

BUCKWHEAT OMELETTE

Serves 2 as a main meal, 4 as a light meal

This recipe is from Japan where buckwheat flour is commonly used to make noodles. If buckwheat flour is unavailable you can use wholemeal flour.

4 oz (100 g) buckwheat flour	1 green pepper, seeded, cored and diced
4 eggs, lightly beaten	4 oz (100 g) mushrooms, sliced
4 fl oz (100 ml) water	black pepper to taste
1 tablespoon (15 ml) soya sauce	2 tablespoons (30 ml) vegetable oil
1 small onion, diced	

Beat the flour, eggs, water and soya sauce into a smooth batter and then stir in all the remaining ingredients, except the oil. Heat half the oil in a frying pan and ladle in half the batter mixture. Cook on both sides over a moderate heat until nicely browned. The vegetables should remain slightly crunchy in texture. Repeat for the remaining batter.

PIPERADE

Serves 4

This is a colourful egg dish from the Basque region of France. It is quick to make and the ingredients are usually readily available. Serve it hot with wholemeal toast for that unexpected lunch. Be careful not to overcook the eggs.

30 ml (2 tablespoons) vegetable oil (olive oil if possible)	salt and black pepper to taste
450 g (1 lb) onions, finely sliced	6 medium eggs, beaten
2 large red or green peppers, cored, seeded and sliced	fresh basil, finely chopped or dried basil, to garnish
450 g (1 lb) ripe tomatoes, peeled and chopped or use tinned tomatoes, drained	

Heat the oil in a large frying pan (with a lid available) over a moderate heat. Add the onion and cook with stirring until just softened. Add the peppers and continue cooking and stirring until they are softened. Stir in the tomatoes and salt and black pepper to taste. Cover the pan and gently cook over a low heat for 7-8 minutes. The mixture should be just moist rather than sloppy. If it's too wet, remove the lid of the pan and simmer off some liquid. Pour in the beaten eggs and stir continuously until the egg is lightly set (as you would scrambled eggs). Sprinkle with basil and serve immediately with hot wholemeal toast.

CHATCHOUKA (EGGS WITH TOMATOES)

Serves 4

Chatchouka is a dish of North African origin. It was taken to Spain during the Arab invasions and is said to be the basis of Spanish omelette. Chatchouka is popular throughout the Middle East.

2 tablespoons (30 ml) vegetable oil	18 oz (500 g) small tomatoes, halved
2 medium green peppers, decored, seeded, thinly sliced	salt and black pepper to taste
½-1 red chilli pepper, finely chopped (optional)	6 medium eggs
2 medium onions, diced	fresh parsley, finely chopped for garnishing
2 cloves garlic, crushed	

Heat the oil in a heavy or non–stick frying pan and add the green peppers, chilli pepper, onions and garlic. Stir–fry until the onion is softened and lightly coloured. Add the tomatoes and cook gently with occasional stirring until they are very soft. Season to taste with salt and black pepper. Break the eggs over the surface of the contents of the frying pan and gently stir them with a wooden spoon to break the yolks. Cook with occasional stirring until the chatchouka is set. Serve garnished with parsley.

BOMBAY EGGS   *Serves 6 as a snack, 3 as a main meal*

These are hard-boiled eggs wrapped in a lentil coating and deep-fried. They are rich in protein. Serve 1 per person with bread and pickles as a snack, or 2 per person served with a salad as a main dish.

2 large onions, diced	1 teaspoon turmeric
8 oz (225 g) brown lentils	salt and black pepper to taste
2 tablespoons (30 ml) vegetable oil	6 hard-boiled eggs, shelled
2 tablespoons (30 ml) grated Cheddar cheese	plain flour for dusting
2 tablespoons (30 ml) fresh coriander leaves or parsley, finely chopped	2 eggs, beaten
	wholemeal breadcrumbs for coating
1-2 teaspoons curry powder (depending on personal taste)	oil for deep-frying

Put the onions and lentils in a large pan and mix well together. Cover them well with water, bring it to the boil and simmer for 1-1½ hours or until the lentils are very soft. Drain well, reserving the liquid for soup-making. Heat the oil in a frying pan, add the onions and lentils, stir continuously over a low heat, until all the moisture has evaporated and you are left with a fairly thick mixture. Add the cheese, coriander, curry powder (to taste), turmeric, salt and pepper, and mix well. Cool. Now divide the mixture into 6 equal portions and use each portion to coat one egg completely. Dust the coated eggs with seasoned flour, dip each into the beaten egg and then roll in breadcrumbs. Heat the oil for deep-frying until it just starts to smoke. Deep-fry the coated eggs three at a time, until their coating is crisp and golden.

POTATO, CHEESE AND ONION PIE
Serves 4

This is a tasty, low fat version of an old favourite.

1 medium onion, thinly sliced

1 tablespoon (15 ml) vegetable oil

3 large potatoes, cooked in their skins for about 10 minutes and then peeled and thinly sliced

2 leeks, cut into rings and par-boiled

4 oz (100 g) curd cheese

2 tablespoons (30 ml) chopped chives

6 tomatoes, seeded and chopped

1 clove garlic, peeled and chopped

salt and pepper to taste

4 tablespoons (60 ml) vegetable stock or water

2 tablespoons grated Parmesan cheese

Preheat the oven to 190°C (375°F, gas mark 5). Fry the onions gently in the oil. Layer the onion, potato slices and leeks in an ovenproof dish with small knobs of curd cheese between each layer. Mix the chives, tomatoes, garlic, salt and pepper and stock or water together. Spoon the mixture over the layers of vegetables. Sprinkle with Parmesan cheese and bake in the preheated oven for 25 minutes.

CHEESE AND OAT BURGERS
Makes 4 Burgers

An alternative to hamburgers, cheese and oat burgers are popular with children. Serve them in a wholemeal bun with a salad for lunch.

6 oz (175 g) Cheddar cheese, grated

1 small green pepper, seeded and finely chopped

1 large tomato, skinned and finely chopped

1 small onion, finely chopped	salt and freshly ground black pepper
4 oz (100 g) porridge oats	
2 eggs	2-4 tablespoons vegetable oil for shallow frying

Reserve 2 oz (50 g) of the cheese for topping. Mix the remaining cheese with the pepper, tomato, onion and oats. Add the eggs and mix thoroughly until well blended. Season generously to taste with salt and black pepper. Divide the mixture into 4 portions and shape each into a burger. If the mixture is a little sticky add more oats so that it binds together well. Heat about 2 tablespoons of oil in a frying pan and gently fry the burgers until golden brown. Turn them carefully with a large spatula and continue cooking until golden brown on the second side. Add a little more oil if necessary. Sprinkle the reserved cheese over the burgers and place under a hot grill until the tops are golden brown.

CHINESE EGGS AND TOMATOES   *Serves 4*

6 eggs	1¼ lbs (550 g) tomatoes, skinned, thickly sliced
1½ tablespoons (25 ml) rice wine or sherry (or cider vinegar plus 1 teaspoon honey)	4 tablespoons (60 ml) vegetable stock or milk
pinch salt	2 spring onions, finely chopped
2 tablespoons (30 ml) vegetable oil	

Beat the eggs with the rice wine and salt. Heat the oil in a frying pan. Fry the tomato slices over a moderate heat. Add a little salt and then the beaten egg mixture. Stir-fry for 1-2 minutes, as for scrambled eggs. Pour in the stock and cook for a further minute. Serve immediately, very hot, sprinkled with the chopped spring onion.

LEEKS AND NOODLES BAKED WITH CHEESE

Serves 4

This is a filling and nutritious meal that looks and tastes good enough to serve at a dinner party.

2 tablespoons (30 ml) vegetable oil	12 oz (350 g) wholewheat tagliatelle or noodles, cooked
1 large onion, finely chopped	
2 bunches watercress, washed, stalks removed	2 oz (50 g) Parmesan cheese
	2 oz (50 g) butter
1½ lb (700 g) leeks, washed, sliced thinly	2 oz (50 g) wholemeal flour
	16 fl oz (450 ml) milk
salt and black pepper	4 oz (100 g) wholewheat breadcrumbs
2 eggs, lightly beaten	

Heat the oil in a saucepan, add the onion, watercress and leeks. Cook gently for 10-15 minutes, stirring occasionally until tender. Season with salt and black pepper. Stir in the eggs, mixing well. Arrange half the cooked tagliatelle in a baking dish. Sprinkle half the Parmesan cheese over this and cover it with half the leek and watercress mixture. Add layers of the remaining tagliatelle, Parmesan and watercress and leek mixture.

Preheat the oven to 400°F (200°C, gas mark 6). Melt the butter in a saucepan, add the flour and cook for one minute. Gradually add the milk and bring to the boil, stirring continuously until the sauce is thick and smooth. Season with salt and black pepper and pour over the top of the layers in the baking dish. Sprinkle the breadcrumbs over the dish and bake in the preheated oven for 20-25 minutes or until golden brown. Serve straight from the baking dish.

BULGAR WHEAT CHEESE GRATIN

Serves 4

2 tablespoons (30 ml) vegetable oil

1 medium onion, diced

1 medium green pepper, cored, seeded and diced

4 oz (100 g) mushrooms, sliced

8 oz (225 g) coarse bulgar wheat, cooked (see page 25)

8 fl oz (225 ml) BÉCHAMEL SAUCE (see page 197)

4 oz (100 g) cheese, grated

Preheat the oven to 375°F (190°C, gas mark 5). Heat the oil in a heavy pan, sauté the onion and green pepper until just soft, stir in the mushrooms and cook for a further 2–3 minutes. Place the cooked bulgar wheat in a casserole dish, cover it with the onion, pepper and mushroom mixture, pour the béchamel sauce over the dish, sprinkle with grated cheese and bake uncovered in the preheated oven for 30 minutes or until nicely browned.

GRATIN OF POTATOES AND MUSHROOMS

Serves 4

This is a creamy dish. Serve it with steamed vegetables and a simple salad.

2 oz (50 g) butter

1 clove garlic, cut in half

1 lb (450 g) potatoes, peeled and thinly sliced

salt and freshly ground black pepper

8 oz (225 g) mushrooms, sliced

4 fl oz (100 ml) fresh cream

4 fl oz (100 ml) milk

6 oz (175 g) Mozzarella cheese, sliced

Preheat the oven to 350°F (180°C, gas mark 4). Rub the base and sides of an oval gratin dish with half the butter and the garlic clove. Arrange half the potato slices in the bottom of the dish and season with salt and black pepper. Layer the mushroom slices on top and then the remainder of the potato. Season again. Combine the cream and milk and pour into the dish. Dot the top of the potatoes with the remaining butter. Cover the top with the Mozzarella cheese slices and bake for 1 hour 15 minutes until the potatoes are cooked and the top is golden brown.

WATERCRESS (OR SPINACH) AND ONION QUICHE

Serves 4

If watercress is unavailable, use 1 lb (450 g) fresh spinach instead.

PASTRY

6 oz (175 g) wholemeal flour	pinch of salt
2 oz (50 g) plain flour	4 oz (100 g) vegetable margarine

FILLING

1 tablespoon (15 ml) vegetable oil	2 oz (50 g) Parmesan cheese
1 small onion, finely chopped	5 fl oz (150 ml) milk
6 bunches of watercress, washed, stalks removed	½ teaspoon freshly grated nutmeg
6 oz (175 g) cottage cheese	salt and pepper
3 eggs, beaten	

Place the flours and salt in a large mixing bowl and rub in the margarine until the mixture resembles breadcrumbs. Sprinkle 2-3 tablespoons (30–40 ml) iced water over the mixture and mix to a firm dough. On a lightly floured board, roll out the pastry thinly and use it to line an 8 in (20 cm) flan ring. Chill for 30 minutes. Preheat the oven to 375°F (190°C, gas mark 5).

Meanwhile, make the filling. Heat the oil in a saucepan over a medium heat, add the onion and cook until soft, but not coloured. Add the watercress and cook for a further 2 minutes or until the leaves are just soft. Cool slightly, add the cottage cheese, eggs, Parmesan and milk, and season with nutmeg, salt and pepper. Mix well.

Pour this filling mixture into the prepared flan case and bake in the preheated oven for 35 minutes, or until the centre of the flan is just firm and the top is golden. It can be served hot or cold.

COURGETTE AND TOMATO
CHEESE FLAN

Serves 6

A simple and convenient dish to make for lunch or a light dinner. If fresh herbs are available, they will lift its flavour to something special. For the occasional treat replace the milk with single cream.

1 recipe quantity wholewheat shortcrust pastry (see recipe for WATERCRESS AND ONION QUICHE, page 141)

8 oz (225 g) courgettes

1 oz (25 g) butter

2 gloves garlic, crushed

4 tomatoes, skinned and thinly sliced

2 eggs

¼ pint (150 g) milk (or single cream)

3 oz (75 g) Cheddar, grated

salt and black pepper to taste

2 teaspoons fresh basil or ½ teaspoon dried basil

2 teaspoons fresh oregano or ½ teaspoon dried oregano

Roll out the pastry thinly on a lightly floured surface and use it to line a 9 in (22.5 cm) flan dish. Prick the base and chill until required. Pre-heat oven to 190°C (375°F, gas mark 5).

Wash and slice the courgettes. Melt the butter in a pan, add the courgettes and garlic and cook for a few minutes until the courgettes begin to soften. Arrange the courgettes with the tomato slices in the flan case.

Beat together the eggs, milk or cream and cheese. Add seasoning to taste and the oregano and basil. Pour this mixture over courgettes and tomatoes. Bake in the preheated oven for 40–45 minutes or until the filling is set and golden brown on top. Serve hot or cold.

CHEESE PIE IN MINUTES   *Serves 4*

This dish can be prepared in a flash! Everything is whizzed in the blender. It is very tasty and highly satisfying if served with a green vegetable.

1 small onion, roughly chopped	1 teaspoon Dijon mustard
4 oz (100 g) wholemeal breadcrumbs	¾ pint (450 ml) milk
4 oz (100 g) hard cheese, grated	salt and black pepper to taste
2 eggs	

Preheat the oven to 400°F (200°C, gas mark 6). Put all the ingredients in a liquidizer and blend until smooth. Pour the mixture into a greased shallow baking dish. Bake for about 45 minutes until set and golden brown. Serve hot from the dish.

TOMATOES BAKED WITH CHEESE   *Serves 4*

The tomatoes are just softened with the cheese melting into them. The parsley stays bright green. With an added jacket potato this makes a good lunch dish. Courgettes, marrow, mushrooms, blanched leeks, in fact most vegetables, may be substituted for the tomatoes.

4 large beef tomatoes or 1½ lbs (675 g) normal tomatoes	4 tablespoons (60 ml) chopped green parsley
knob of low-fat margarine	4 oz (100 g) hard cheese, grated

Preheat the oven to 400°F (200°C, gas mark 6). Wipe and slice the tomatoes thickly. Lay them in a large oven-proof dish, greased with the margarine. Scatter over the parsley, then the cheese over the top. Cover the dish with foil. Bake in the preheated oven for 30 minutes. Serve hot.

RED PEPPER AND COTTAGE CHEESE GRATIN
Serves 4

A light, easy to prepare meal, low in calories. More akin to a soufflé than anything else. Serve with crusty bread and your favourite salad.

1 oz (25 g) wholemeal breadcrumbs	2 medium-size red peppers, de-seeded, finely chopped
½ oz (15 g) low-fat margarine	1 teaspoon dried thyme
1 large onion, sliced thinly	8 oz (225 g) cottage cheese
1 clove garlic, chopped	4 eggs, separated

Preheat oven to 375°F (190°C, gas mark 5). Grease a deep gratin dish and coat the inside with the breadcrumbs. Melt the margarine in a saucepan over a low heat, add the onion and garlic and cook till they just turn golden. Add the peppers, cover and cook for 8–10 minutes. Take off the heat and leave to cool. In a large bowl mix the herbs into the cheese and beat in the egg yolks. Then mix in the cooked pepper, onion and garlic mixture. Stiffly whip the egg whites and add these by gently folding in. Quickly pile into the prepared gratin dish. Bake for 35 minutes in the preheated oven and serve immediately.

PAN HAGGARTY
Serves 4

This is a simple variation of the traditional Northumbrian dish, traditionally cooked on top of a fire in a big frying pan.

6 large potatoes	½ teaspoon dried sage
1 large onion, thinly sliced	½ pint (275 ml) vegetable stock (made with 1 vegetable stock cube)
6 oz (175 g) Cheddar cheese, grated	
salt and black pepper to taste	

Preheat the oven to 350°F (180°C, gas mark 4). Scrub the potatoes and boil them in their jackets until nearly cooked. When cool, peel off their skins and cut them into ¼ in (0.5 cm) slices. Place onions, grated cheese and potato slices in a deep casserole, in layers, seasoning each layer with the dried sage, salt and pepper. Pour over the stock. Bake in the preheated oven for about 30 minutes or until the top is golden brown. Serve with a green vegetable or your favourite salad.

STUFFED TOMATOES AND CHEESE BALLS

The following two recipes go well individually or together. Served alone, the stuffed tomatoes make an unusual accompaniment to a main dish of grains and a sauce, or they could be served with salad and bread as a light meal. The cheese and nut balls are good in a tomato sauce with spaghetti. Alternatively, prepare both dishes together and bake in the same oven. Served together with a simple green salad and bread, they are excellent.

TOMATOES WITH WALNUT AND COTTAGE CHEESE FILLING
Serves 4

4 large firm tomatoes	1 tablespoon (15 ml) freshly diced onion
4 oz (100 g) cottage cheese	½ teaspoon dried thyme
2 oz (50 g) chopped walnuts	salt and black pepper to taste
2 oz (50 g) wholemeal breadcrumbs	1 tablespoon (15 ml) vegetable oil

Preheat the oven to 350°F (180°C, gas mark 4). Cut ½ in (1 cm) tops off the tomatoes and scoop out the flesh leaving a ½ in (1 cm) shell. Sprinkle the inside of each shell with a little salt and black pepper. Combine the cottage cheese, walnuts, breadcrumbs, onion, thyme, salt and black pepper and mix well. Stuff the tomatoes with the mixture and press the tops back into place. Brush the tomatoes with oil and put them on a greased baking sheet. Bake in the preheated oven for 30–35 minutes.

CHEESE AND NUT BALLS   *Serves 4*

2 tablespoons (30 ml) vegetable oil	4 oz (100 g) cheese, grated
1 medium onion, finely diced	2 teaspoons soya sauce
2 cloves garlic, crushed	black pepper to taste
8 oz (225 g) ground mixed nuts	2 eggs, beaten
8 oz (225 g) wholemeal breadcrumbs	

Sauté the onion and garlic in the oil until softened. Remove them from the heat, stir in the ground nuts and breadcrumbs and leave this mixture on one side. Combine the cheese, soya sauce, pepper and beaten eggs in a bowl and mix well. Stir in the nut mixture and mix thoroughly. Preheat the oven to 350°F (180°C, gas mark 4). Form the mixture into 2 in (5 cm) balls (this is easier with wet hands) and place these on a greased baking sheet. Bake for 10–12 minutes on one side and then turn the balls over and bake for a further 10–12 minutes or until brown and firm.

COURGETTE EGGAH   *Serves 4-6*

This delicious egg dish is thick and well filled. It is baked, cooled and then cut into thin wedges. It is rich in eggs and butter and is best eaten in moderate amounts, when it will do you good rather than harm.

100 g (4 oz) butter	9 eggs, lightly beaten
1 large onion, finely chopped	2 tablespoons (30 ml) fresh parsley, finely chopped
2 cloves garlic, crushed	½ teaspoon turmeric
450 g (1 lb) courgettes, thinly sliced	salt and freshly ground black pepper to taste

Melt the butter in a heavy frying pan and sauté the onion and garlic until softened. Add the courgettes and cook over a medium heat, stirring, until the courgettes are lightly browned and all the moisture has evaporated from the pan. Allow the mixture to cool and transfer it to a bowl. Stir in the eggs, parsley, turmeric and salt and black pepper to taste. Preheat the oven to 375°F (190°C, gas mark 5). Pour the mixture into a greased 9 in (23 cm) non-stick casserole dish and bake in the preheated oven for 30 minutes or until nicely set. Remove the dish from the oven and if you wish brown the top under a hot grill. Allow to cool. Turn the eggah onto a serving dish and cut into thin wedges.

LETTUCE SOUFFLÉ   *Serves 4*

This low-fat, elegant dish is just right for a healthy dinner party.

2 oz (50 g) grated Parmesan cheese	¼ pint (150 ml) semi-skimmed milk
8 oz (225 g) Iceberg lettuce, chopped	1 teaspoon Worcestershire sauce
2 oz (50 g) butter or vegetable margarine	4 oz (100 g) Cheddar cheese, grated
¾ oz (20 g) flour	4 eggs, separated
salt and freshly ground black pepper to taste	¾ teaspoon cream of tartar

Preheat the oven to 375°F (190°C, gas mark 5). Prepare a 7 in (18 cm) soufflé dish (or other deep dish) by buttering and coating the inside with most of the Parmesan. Simmer the chopped lettuce in very little water until just tender, then drain. Add ½ oz (12.5 g) butter or margarine and cook, stirring, until all moisture has disappeared. In a separate pan, melt the remaining butter, blend in the flour, salt and black pepper. Cook over a low heat for 3–5 minutes. Blend in the milk and

Worcestershire sauce. Cook and stir until thickened. Remove from the heat. Add the Cheddar cheese and stir in until melted. Beat in the egg yolks one at a time, then add the cooked lettuce. Beat the egg whites until foamy, add the cream of tartar and a pinch of salt, then whip until stiff. Gently fold the egg whites, a little at a time, into the lettuce mixture. Pour into the prepared soufflé dish and smooth the top. Sprinkle with the remaining Parmesan. Bake in the middle of the preheated oven for 30–40 minutes, until well risen and golden brown. Serve immediately.

BEANCURD AND CHEESE MUSHROOM OMELETTE
Serves 2

This is a high protein combination of Eastern cheese (beancurd) and English cheddar.

2 eggs	4 oz (100 g) Cheddar cheese, grated
2 tablespoons (30 ml) natural yoghurt	1 teaspoon vegetable oil
4 oz (100 g) beancurd (see page 31)	4 oz (100 g) mushrooms, chopped

Blend or beat together the eggs, yoghurt, beancurd and cheese. Heat the oil in a frying pan and gently sauté the mushrooms. Pour in the egg mixture and cook over a low heat until firm on the bottom. Fold the omelette in half in the pan, cook a little longer, until set to your liking, and then serve.

PANCAKES

Once the batter is prepared and stored in the fridge, pancakes are easy to make for a quick sweet or savoury snack. Here is a basic recipe, followed by one that uses buckwheat flour. Buckwheat is an Eastern European ingredient and the flour is obtained from the crushed seeds of the buckwheat plant. Serve pancakes on their own with honey and lemon juice or stuffed with left-over cooked grains, pulses and vegetables.

BASIC BATTER AND METHOD   *Makes 8 pancakes*

4 oz (100 g) plain wholemeal flour	pinch of salt
1 large egg	vegetable oil or butter for frying
½ pint (300 ml) semi-skimmed milk	

Place all but the oil or butter in a food processor or blender and mix to form a smooth batter. Alternatively, sieve the flour and salt into a bowl (return to the flour any bran from the sieve), make a well in the centre and add the egg. Add half the milk a little at a time and beat the mixture until smooth. Stir in the remaining milk to make a smooth, runny batter. Transfer batter to a pouring jug.

Place a 7-8 in (18-22 cm) frying pan (thick-based pans are best) over a medium heat, brush the inside surface with a little oil or butter to form a thin film of fat and then spoon or pour in enough batter to cover the base of the pan. Quickly move the pan to and fro to ensure all the base is covered. Pour any excess batter back into the jug. Cook the pancakes over a moderate heat for about 1 minute each side or until golden. Turn them over with a palette knife or, if you are brave, by tossing them. If you are making a lot of pancakes for immediate use serve them as made or keep them hot stacked between two plates in a warm oven. Cold pancakes can be reheated in a hot frying pan without any oil or butter.

BUCKWHEAT PANCAKES   *Makes 8 small pancakes*

3 oz (75 g) plain wholemeal flour	salt to taste
1 oz (25 g) buckwheat flour	8-10 fl oz (225-275 ml) cold water
1 tablespoon (15 ml) soya flour	vegetable oil for frying

Combine the flours and salt in a bowl. Mix in the cold water to form a medium–stiff batter. Beat the batter well and then leave it to stand for 30 minutes. Beat the batter again and drop tablespoonsful of the amount into a small, oiled, hot frying pan. Turn when set and brown the underside.

GRAINS AND PASTA

RICE CROQUETTES

Serves 4

This is a good recipe for using up left-over cooked vegetables and/or cooked rice.

1 lb (450 g) short or long grain cooked rice, drained (see pages 24 and 25)

2 medium onions and 2 medium carrots, finely chopped or 1 lb (450 g) mixed cooked vegetables

4 oz (100 g) wholemeal flour

salt and black pepper to taste

2 eggs, beaten

wholemeal breadcrumbs or flour for coating

oil for frying

Parmesan cheese or grated Cheddar cheese, to garnish

parsley, chopped, to garnish

Combine the rice with the onions and carrots or cooked vegetables, the flour, seasoning and beaten eggs and mix well. Wet your hands in cold water and form the mixture into 8 croquettes. Keeping your hands wet stops the mixture sticking to them. Roll the croquettes in breadcrumbs or flour. Now shallow-fry them for about 5 minutes on both sides over a low heat or until nicely browned. Alternatively, deep-fry them in hot oil for 3-4 minutes. Serve garnished with a sprinkling of cheese and parsley.

APPLES AND RICE WITH ONIONS
Serves 4

This is good as an accompaniment to a main dish or on its own with cheese and salad.

2 medium onions, sliced	1 lb (450 g) cooking apples, peeled or unpeeled, sliced
1 tablespoon (15 ml) vegetable oil	
3 oz (75 g) long grain rice	2 oz (50 g) sugar or honey
5 fl oz (125 ml) water	

In a large pan, brown the sliced onions in the oil, stirring until just golden. Add the rice and water and cook slowly. After the water has boiled, reduce the heat and let simmer until the rice is cooked (about 20 minutes for white rice; 40–50 minutes for brown rice). Watch it in the last few minutes – all the liquid should have gone and the rice could burn quickly after this point. If the rice is not done when the liquid is gone, add a little more water and cook longer as necessary.

While the rice is cooking, cook the apple until soft in as little water as possible. Add the sugar or honey to sweeten at the end of the cooking. Keep warm until the rice is ready. Then mix the rice well so that the onions are distributed throughout. Pile the rice with onions on a platter bordered with the hot cooked apples and serve.

TEA AND RICE (CHAZUKE)
Serves 1

This is a quick snack and a favourite Japanese method of using up left-over rice. Green tea is normally used but you could try your own favourite brand or flavour.

8 oz (225 g) cooked rice (see pages 24 and 25)	1 sheet nori
8 fl oz (225 ml) hot green tea	

Place the rice in individual bowls. Pour over the hot tea. Wave a sheet of nori over a medium gas flame or hot plate for 30–40 seconds until crisp and then crumble it over the tea and rice.

SIMPLE FRIED RICE

Serves 4

This well-known Chinese dish is a really excellent way of using up any left-over rice or vegetables. It is best cooked very fast in a wok, but if you haven't got one use a large, heavy frying pan over a high heat.

2 tablespoons (30 ml) vegetable oil	2 eggs, beaten
1 lb (450 g) cooked rice (see pages 24 and 25)	2-3 spring onions, chopped
	soya sauce

Heat the oil in a heavy frying pan or wok over a high heat. Put the rice in the pan and stir-fry for 2-3 minutes. Reduce the heat and pour in the eggs. Stir-fry for a further 4-5 minutes. Transfer from the pan to a serving dish, sprinkle the spring onions and soya sauce over the top. Serve.

SIMPLE PILAU RICE

Serves 4

4 tablespoons (60 ml) olive oil	salt and black pepper to taste
½ teaspoon crushed saffron or 1 teaspoon turmeric	2 oz (50 g) pine nuts or almonds, blanched
1 lb (450 g) long grain white rice, washed and drained	2 medium onions, sliced

Heat half the oil in a heavy frying pan and stir in the saffron or turmeric. Measure out the rice in cupfuls and note how many there are. Put the rice into the frying pan and fry, stirring until all the rice is coated with oil and slightly tinted yellow. Remove the pan from the heat. Pour into the pan boiling water equal to 1½ volumes of the rice. Season to taste with salt and pepper. Bring to the boil, reduce the heat, cover and simmer for 20 minutes or until all the moisture is absorbed and the rice is tender. Meanwhile, in another pan fry the pine nuts in the remaining oil until they are lightly browned, add the onions and stir-fry until they are softened. Serve the rice in a mound with the onions and pine nuts sprinkled over the top.

GREEN RICE

Serves 4-6

1 lb (450 g) long grain rice, washed, drained

8 oz (225 g) spinach, washed and drained, or 1 large bunch of watercress, washed and drained

salt to taste

Cook the rice by the basic method (see pages 24 and 25). While it is cooking prepare the spinach or watercress by blanching it briefly in a pan of boiling water. As soon as the leaves soften rinse them under cold water. Drain well and gently press out as much moisture as you can. Cut the greens into shreds, salt to taste and stir them into the cooked rice before serving.

CHEESE RICE CAKES

Serves 4

4 oz (100 g) cheese, finely grated

4 oz (100 g) cottage cheese

1 small onion, finely diced

2 eggs beaten

1 tablespoon (15 ml) wholemeal flour

¼ teaspoon nutmeg

½ teaspoon cinnamon

salt and pepper to taste

6 oz (175 g) cooked white rice, drained (see pages 24 and 25)

wholemeal breadcrumbs or flour for coating

oil for shallow frying

Combine the cheese, onion and half the beaten egg in a mixing bowl and stir well together. Add the flour, nutmeg, cinnamon and salt and pepper to taste. Mix well by hand. Mix in the drained rice and more flour slowly if the mixture is not firm enough to hold its shape. Shape the mixture into about 10 round cakes. This is easier if you clean your hands after making the mixture and then keep them wet while you shape the cakes. Dip the rice cakes into the remaining beaten egg and roll them in breadcrumbs or flour. Heat the oil in a frying pan and gently fry the rice cakes until nicely browned on both sides (about 5 minutes each side). Keep cooked cakes warm under a low grill whilst frying the remainder.

YELLOW RICE WITH SPICES *Serves 4-6*

1 lb (450 g) long grain white rice, washed several times and drained	1 teaspoon ground coriander
	½ teaspoon ground cumin
2 tablespoons (30 ml) vegetable oil	½ teaspoon cinnamon
	salt to taste
1 small onion, finely diced	1 pint (550 ml) water, boiling
1 teaspoon ground turmeric	

Put the rice in a bowl, cover it with water and leave it to soak for 2-3 hours. Drain it then set the rice aside. Heat the vegetable oil in a heavy-bottomed pan and stir-fry the onion in it until softened. Add the spices and salt and sauté the mixture for another minute. Stir the rice into the pan and sauté the rice, onion and spices for 2-3 minutes. Pour in the boiling water and cook the rice over a moderate heat until all the water is absorbed. Stir the rice with the handle end of a wooden spoon and cover the pot with a tightly fitting lid. Reduce the heat to very low, gently cook the rice for another 15 minutes and then serve.

RED RICE *Serves 4*

Here rice and aduki beans eaten together provide a rich protein source as well as a colourful dish.

4 oz (100 g) aduki beans, soaked in water for 6 hours or more	1 teaspoon salt
	2 tablespoons (30 ml) sesame seeds, toasted
2 pints (1.1 litres) water	
1 lb (450 g) long grain brown rice, washed, drained	

Drain the soaked beans. Place them in a large pan with the water, bring them to the boil, reduce the heat, then cover and simmer until cooked (about 1½ hours). Drain, put the beans to one side and reserve the cooking liquid. Put the rice in the pan, add more water to the bean cooking liquid to make up to 1½ pints (850 ml) and add this to the rice. Cover and bring to the boil. Reduce the heat and simmer, covered, for 30 minutes. Now add the drained beans, mix well and continue to simmer until the rice is cooked (a further 20 minutes). Combine the salt and toasted sesame seeds. Serve the red rice hot or cold, garnished with the sesame seed and salt mixture (a Japanese condiment known as *gomasio*).

THAI FRIED RICE   *Serves 4*

Fried rice is a convenient method of using up cold left-over cooked rice, which anyway fries much better than freshly cooked rice. Do make sure, however, the cooked rice smells fresh and is safe to use. Fried rice is a dish to improvise with and the method given here is only one of many. In the Thai manner it is 'hot' and also flavoured with coriander leaves.

3 tablespoons (45 ml) vegetable oil	2 tablespoons (30 ml) soya sauce
2 cloves garlic, finely chopped	1 lb (450 g) cooked rice (see pages 24 and 25)
1 medium onion, finely chopped	2 tablespoons (30 ml) tomato purée
1 red or green chilli pepper, seeded and chopped (reduce amount if you like mild food)	1 small or ½ medium cucumber, sliced
1 in (2.5 cm) piece root ginger, peeled and cut into fine slivers	2 tablespoons (30 ml) chopped coriander leaves

Heat the oil in a wok or large saucepan. Add the garlic and onion and fry until the onion is softened. Add the chilli pepper and ginger and stir-fry for 2 minutes. Add the soya sauce, stir well and then add the rice and tomato purée. Stir-fry until the rice is well heated through. Transfer to a serving dish. Surround the edge of the plate with cucumber slices and garnish the rice with coriander leaves. Serve immediately.

RICE AND LENTIL PILAU *Serves 4*

Pilau is the Indian equivalent of the Arab pilaff or the Spanish paella. It is essentially a dish of rice cooked with other ingredients in the same pot. The recipe given here may be used as a basis for your own improvisations, using different pulses, spices or vegetables.

3 tablespoons (45 ml) vegetable oil	1 tablespoon (15 ml) tomato purée
1 medium onion, chopped	½ teaspoon cumin seeds
8 oz (225 g) long grain, brown rice	½ teaspoon coriander seeds, crushed
1 pint (575 ml) water or vegetable stock	½ teaspoon cinnamon
	4 oz (100 g) raisins
8 oz (225 g) brown lentils, soaked 3-4 hours, drained	4 oz (100 g) sunflower seeds
	salt to taste

Heat the oil in a heavy pan and sauté the onion until softened. Stir in the rice and cook, stirring, for 3-4 minutes. Add the remaining ingredients and mix well. Bring to the boil, cover the pot, reduce the heat and simmer for 50 minutes to 1 hour or until the rice is tender and the lentils are cooked.

SWEET SMELLING COCONUT RICE
Serves 4-6

This delicious South-East Asian rice dish is simple to prepare and it gives an exotic aroma to even the simplest meal.

1¼ pints (700 ml) coconut milk	½ teaspoon cinnamon
1½ teaspoons salt	1 teaspoon grated lemon rind or chopped lemon grass
¼ teaspoon freshly ground black pepper	1 bay leaf
¼ teaspoon ground cloves	1 lb (450 g) long grain, white rice
½ teaspoon nutmeg	

Put all the ingredients except the rice into a heavy saucepan and bring the mixture to a gentle boil, stirring constantly. Add the rice and bring to a very slow boil, stirring. Cover the pan with a tightly fitting lid, reduce the heat and simmer for 20 minutes. Remove the pan from the heat, stir and then set aside, off the heat, for 5 minutes before serving.

CASHEW AND ALMOND PILAU
Serves 4

In this Indian recipe some of the spices are left whole. They are not removed after cooking, but neither are they eaten.

3 tablespoons (45 ml) vegetable oil	12 oz (350 g) long grain rice (brown or white)
1 in (2.5 cm) piece cinnamon	1½ pints (900 ml) water, boiling
3 cloves	2 oz (50 g) almonds, blanched
3 cardamom seeds	2 oz (50 g) cashews, lightly roasted
6 peppercorns	2 oz (50 g) sultanas
½ teaspoon cumin seeds	

Heat the oil in a heavy pan and fry the cinnamon, cloves, cardamoms, peppercorns and cumin seeds for 2–3 minutes. Add the rice and stir-fry for 2–3 minutes. Pour in the water, reduce the heat, cover and simmer until the rice is nearly tender (20–25 minutes for white rice, 40–45 minutes for brown rice). Now stir in the nuts and sultanas, re-cover the pot and cook until the rice is tender.

PLAIN BUCKWHEAT (KASHA)   *Serves 3-4*

Buckwheat may be served instead of rice with vegetables or sauces. It is also delicious on its own.

8 oz (225 g) buckwheat	½ teaspoon salt
16 fl oz (450 ml) boiling water	2 oz (50 g) butter

Toast the buckwheat in a heavy, dry saucepan over a medium heat until it turns a deep colour and starts to smell nutty. Stir constantly to prevent it from burning. Pour over the boiling water, add the salt and cover. Reduce the heat and simmer for 15–20 minutes or until all the water has been absorbed and the buckwheat is tender. Stir in the butter and serve.

BUCKWHEAT (KASHA) CROQUETTES
Serves 4

8 oz (225 g) buckwheat, cooked as in previous recipe	1 tablespoon (15 ml) soya sauce
2 oz (50 g) wholewheat flour	water
1 onion, finely diced	oil for frying
4 oz (100 g) cooked vegetables, finely chopped or cooked beans or mushrooms, finely chopped	

Combine the buckwheat with the flour, onion, vegetables and soya sauce. Mix in enough water (if needed) to form a firm mixture that will hold its shape. Form this mixture into balls about 2 in (5 cm) in diameter or into burger shapes. Deep-fry the balls in hot oil until golden brown or shallow-fry the burgers in a little oil in a heavy frying pan, browning on both sides.

PLAIN BULGAR WHEAT   *Serves 3-4*

Bulgar wheat is prepared by parboiling wholewheat grains in a minimum amount of water. The wheat is then spread thinly on a cloth or tray, dried out (traditionally in the sun) and finally cracked between stone rollers. It can be bought in various grades ranging from fine to coarsely cracked.

It is cooked by steaming or boiling, sometimes being dry roasted first. Some makes are roasted and parboiled before packaging, to give a fast-cooking product. Fine bulgar wheat cooks in 20–30 minutes if just covered in very hot water and set aside. It may be served instead of rice with vegetables or sauces, or as the basis for a cold salad.

8 oz (225 g) coarse bulgar wheat

16 fl oz (450 ml) water

salt to taste

Dry roast the bulgar in a heavy saucepan over a medium heat for 2–3 minutes, stirring constantly. Remove from the heat, allow to cool for a couple of minutes and then add the water. Bring to the boil, reduce the heat, cover and simmer for 15 minutes or until all the water is absorbed. Salt to taste towards the end of the cooking time.

BULGAR WHEAT, VEGETABLE AND BEAN CASSEROLE *Serves 4*

This casserole contains an excellent combination of complementary food stuffs. Served with a green salad it constitutes a complete meal. For speed and convenience use tinned beans or left-over cooked beans.

8 oz (225 g) coarse bulgar wheat	3 tomatoes, scalded, peeled and chopped
¾ pint (450 ml) water	1 tablespoon (15 ml) tomato purée
1 medium onion, chopped	
2 tablespoons (30 ml) vegetable oil	2 tablespoons (30 ml) soya sauce
1 carrot, scrubbed and sliced	4 oz (100 g) of a single bean or a bean mix, soaked and cooked until tender, then drained or 8 oz (225 g) tinned red beans or chickpeas
1 green pepper, seeded, cored and chopped	
4 oz (100 g) mushrooms, coarsely chopped	

Lightly dry roast the bulgar wheat in a heavy pan, then add the water, cover and simmer for 15 minutes or until the bulgar is just tender. Remove from the heat. Preheat oven to 400°F (200°C, gas mark 6). Sauté the onion in the vegetable oil in an ovenproof pan or casserole dish for 2 minutes. Add the carrot, cover and cook over a moderate heat until the carrot is softened (about 10 minutes). Add the green pepper and mushrooms and cook for a further 2 minutes. Remove the pan from the heat and stir in the tomatoes, tomato purée and soya sauce, then the bulgar wheat and beans. Cover, place in the preheated oven and bake for 20–30 minutes.

BULGAR WHEAT WITH CHEESE AND AUBERGINES   *Serves 4*

This simple dish is easy to prepare and surprisingly tasty, combining three food groups in a nutritious balance.

1 medium aubergine, cut into ¾ in (2 cm) cubes, salted, pressed for 30 minutes, rinsed and drained

2 tablespoons (30 ml) olive oil

8 oz (225 g) coarse bulgar wheat

10 fl oz (300 ml) water

4 oz (100 g) mozzarella or Cheddar cheese, cut into ¾ in (2 cm) cubes

salt and black pepper to taste

Dry the aubergine cubes on kitchen paper or a tea towel. Heat the oil in a frying pan or wok and gently fry the aubergine until just tender. Remove from the pan with a slotted spoon and set aside. Add the bulgar wheat to the pan and stir the wheat over a low heat for a few minutes to lightly coat it with the oil left in the pan. Add the water slowly so that it doesn't spit too much, stir well and simmer until the bulgar wheat is tender (add more water if needed). Add the aubergine cubes, heat through and then stir in the cheese and salt and black pepper to taste. Remove from the heat, set aside covered for 5 minutes and then serve.

BULGAR WHEAT PAELLA   *Serves 4-6*

12 oz (350 g) medium bulgar wheat

2 tablespoons (30 ml) vegetable oil

1 large onion, chopped

1 clove garlic, crushed

2 teaspoons fresh basil, chopped or 1 teaspoon dried basil

1 green pepper, cored, seeded and chopped

1 large carrot, scrubbed and cut into rounds

14 oz (400 g) canned tomatoes, drained and chopped (reserve juice)

4 oz (100 g) mushrooms, quartered

water to make tomato juice up to 1 pint (0.5 litre)

soya sauce to taste

2 tablespoons (30 ml) parsley,
   chopped to garnish

Roast the bulgar wheat in a dry pan over a low heat, stirring occasionally, until golden brown (about 5 minutes). Put the bulgar wheat aside and heat the oil in another large pan. Sauté the onion, garlic and basil for 2 minutes over a low heat. Add the carrot, pepper, tomatoes and mushrooms. Stir well. Cover and cook for a further 5 minutes. Stir in the bulgar wheat, tomato juice and water. Bring to the boil, reduce heat, cover and simmer for 15 minutes. Add soya sauce to taste and serve garnished with parsley.

POLENTA
Serves 4-6

Polenta is a semolina look-alike but it is made from corn rather than wheat grain. In Italy it is cooked into a stiff yellow porridge, itself called polenta. It is served hot, often with a garlicky tomato sauce; or cooled, cut into wedges and fried. Serve with vegetables and/or a salad.

8 oz (225 g) polenta

1¾ pints (1 litre) of gently boiling
   salted water

Pour the polenta slowly into the water in a large pan, stirring continuously. Reduce the heat to the lowest setting and cook, still stirring continuously, for 20 minutes. Once ready the polenta will come away from the sides of the pan. Serve immediately with a sauce of your choice or simply sprinkled with black pepper and olive oil.

Alternatively pour the polenta into an oiled frying pan or other shallow dish, smooth the top, then brush the top with a little olive oil and leave to cool or until solid. Turn the wheel of polenta out of the pan and cut it into wedges. Return the wedges to the pan and fry in olive oil for about 5 minutes each side. Then serve as for freshly cooked polenta.

OAT AND HERB RISSOLES

Serves 4

16 fl oz (450 ml) water	1 tablespoon (15 ml) tomato purée
4 oz (100 g) rolled oats	salt and pepper to taste
1 medium onion, finely chopped	2 eggs, beaten
1 teaspoon dried mixed herbs	wholemeal flour
1 teaspoon dried basil	wholemeal breadcrumbs for coating
1 tablespoon (15 ml) soya sauce	vegetable oil for shallow frying

Bring the water to the boil and stir in the oats. Cook over a low light for 15 minutes, stirring now and again. Add the onion, herbs, soya sauce and tomato purée. Season to taste with salt and black pepper. Add half the beaten egg and enough flour to make a stiff dough. Flour hands and roll the mixture into small rissoles, dip them into the remaining beaten egg and then roll them in the breadcrumbs. Now shallow fry until they are golden brown on both sides.

SWEETCORN AND CHEESE BAKED IN GREEN PEPPERS

Serves 4

4 large green peppers	1 teaspoon dried thyme
12 oz (350 g) fresh corn, cut from the cobs and cooked or 12 oz (350 g) tinned or frozen sweetcorn	½ teaspoon black pepper
	1 teaspoon salt
4 oz (100 g) brown breadcrumbs	8 oz (225 g) cheese, grated

Preheat oven to 375°F (190°C, gas mark 5). Cut the tops off the peppers and deseed. Combine the corn, breadcrumbs, thyme, black pepper, salt and the cheese and mix well. Stuff the peppers with the mixture. Carefully remove the inner stalks from the tops of the peppers and replace the tops on the stuffed peppers. Place the peppers in a casserole and run in hot water to a depth of 1 in (2.5 cm). Cover and bake for 30 minutes or until peppers are tender.

CORN ON THE COB *Serves 4*

Buy the freshest corn you can. To test for freshness press one of the kernels: if it spurts it's fresh.

METHOD 1: BOILED
The following recipe gives the simplest and one of the best ways of preparing corn on the cob. Serve the corn with a good sized knob of butter.

4 ears of corn	pinch basil (optional)
water	butter
salt	

If the corn hasn't already been stripped, remove the husks and silk (to remove the silk hold the ear of corn under a cold running tap and brush with a soft vegetable brush). Bring a large pan of water to the boil (there should be enough water to just cover all the ears of corn), add a pinch of salt and basil, and then drop in the corn. Return the water to the boil and cook the corn for 4–6 minutes or until tender. Drain and serve with a knob of butter.

METHOD 2: BAKED
This method is an excellent way of preparing corn on the cob both at home and out-of-doors on camping trips or at a barbecue when a wood fire or charcoal is used in place of the oven.

4 ears of corn in husks	salt to taste
1 tablespoon (15 ml) vegetable oil or melted butter	

Preheat the oven to 425°F (220°C, gas mark 7). Open the ears of corn by gently turning back the husks. Remove the silk and then brush each ear with oil or butter and sprinkle with salt to taste. Replace the husks, place the cobs on a baking tray and bake in the preheated oven until tender (about 15 minutes). To cook on a fire, allow the flames to die down and place the corn cobs, prepared as above, on the hot embers. Keep turning them and bake for 15–20 minutes.

MILLET WITH ONIONS   *Serves 4*

This is excellent with curried vegetables or add cooked beans for a more substantial dish (see *Variations*).

8 oz (225 g) millet	½ teaspoon black pepper
2 oz (50 g) butter or margarine	1¼ pints (700 ml) boiling water
2 medium onions, diced	2 tablespoons (30 ml) fresh parsley, chopped
1 teaspoon salt	

Put the millet in a heavy pot and dry roast with constant stirring over a medium heat until browned. Add the butter or margarine and onions and sauté the mixture for 2–3 minutes. Add the salt, black pepper and boiling water, cover the pot, reduce the heat and simmer for 30 minutes. Stir in the parsley and serve.

Variations

1 Just before the millet is cooked, stir in 2 oz (50 g) raisins and 4 oz (100 g) mixed nuts and sunflower seeds (or roasted pine nuts or almonds or cashews or a mixture of them are particularly good). Continue cooking and serve when the millet is cooked.

2 Proceed as directed in the recipe above, adding 8 oz (225 g) cooked beans (red beans, chickpeas, haricot beans, aduki beans, etc.) at the same time as the salt, black pepper and water (some or all of the water may be replaced by the liquid the beans were cooked in).

MILLET, CHEESE AND ONION PIE   *Serves 4*

This pie has cheese and onion filling in a wheatflour and millet pastry case.

8 oz (225 g) wholemeal flour	4 medium onions, sliced
4 oz (100 g) millet flakes or flour	8 oz (225 g) cheese, grated
6 oz (175 g) butter or margarine	oregano
water	salt and black pepper
2 tablespoons (30 ml) vegetable oil	

Preheat oven to 375°F (190°C, gas mark 5). Combine the flour and millet flakes or flour and rub in the butter until the mixture resembles breadcrumbs. Add enough water to form a soft pastry. Divide the pastry into 2 equal portions, roll out one half thinly and use it to line a greased 8 in (20 cm) pie dish. Heat the oil in a frying pan and sauté the onions until golden. Layer the cooked onion and cheese in the pie dish and sprinkle a little oregano, salt and black pepper over. Roll out the remaining pastry and use it to cover the pie, sealing the edges by pressing down gently all the way round. Bake in the preheated oven for 30 minutes, until golden brown. Serve hot.

PLAIN BOILED WHOLEWHEAT   *Serves 6*

In most dishes where you would use brown rice, wholewheat can be substituted. It is more fibrous than rice, however, and never cooks to the same softness. It is essential to soak wholewheat grains (also known as berries) for 3–4 hours before cooking.

2 pints (1.1 litres) water	1 teaspoon salt
1 lb (450 g) wholewheat berries, soaked, drained	

Bring the water to a rolling boil. Add the wheat to the boiling water, return mixture to the boil, reduce heat and simmer for 1-1½ hours or until the wheat is cooked to the softness you require. Add salt towards the end of cooking time.

To speed up the cooking time, dry roast the wheat in a hot frying pan for 2-3 minutes before adding to the boiling water.

CHINESE-STYLE WHOLEWHEAT *Serves 4*

2 eggs	2 peppers, diced
1 tablespoon (15 ml) butter	1 lb (450 g) cold, cooked wholewheat (see page 167)
4 tablespoons (60 ml) vegetable oil	4 oz (100 g) mushrooms, diced
1 medium onion, finely chopped	4 teaspoons soya sauce
3 sticks celery, diced	salt and black pepper to taste

Beat the eggs together, heat the butter in a large frying pan, and prepare two thin omelettes. Cut the omelettes into thin strips and set aside. Heat the oil in the frying pan. When it is hot, add the onion, celery and peppers and sauté until just tender. Now add the wholewheat and mushrooms and cook for a further 5 minutes. Just before serving, mix in the omelette strips, soya sauce, salt and black pepper. Serve immediately.

BAKED VEGETABLES AND WHOLEWHEAT   *Serves 4*

8 oz (225 g) wholewheat berries, soaked for 3-4 hours, drained	8 oz (225 g) carrots, finely chopped
1 large onion, sliced	2 medium green peppers, de-seeded
8 oz (225 g) potatoes, peeled, cubed	1 tablespoon (15 ml) tomato purée
4 oz (100 g) mushrooms, sliced (optional)	

4 oz (100 g) wholemeal flour or brown breadcrumbs	1 teaspoon thyme
4 tablespoons (60 ml) vegetable oil	salt and black pepper to taste
	4 oz (100 g) cheese, grated

Boil the wholewheat in plenty of water for 15 minutes. Drain. Preheat oven to 400°F (200°C, gas mark 6). Combine the partially cooked wholewheat with the remaining ingredients, except the cheese, mix well and season to taste. Place the mixture in a deep baking dish or bread tin, sprinkle cheese on top and bake in the preheated oven for 50–60 minutes or until a knife pushed into the centre of the bake comes out clean.

CHEESE, PASTA AND VEGETABLE BAKE

Serves 4

This simple but tasty and nutritious dish is useful for using up left-over cooked pasta.

8 oz (225 g) carrots, thickly sliced	1 oz (25 g) plain flour
8 oz (225 g) celery, coarsely chopped (reserve leaves for garnish)	½ pint (300 ml) milk
	salt and cayenne pepper to taste
8 oz (225 g) cooked wholewheat pasta (see page 23)	1 teaspoon prepared mustard
3 tomatoes, sliced	6 oz (175 g) Cheddar cheese, grated
1 oz (25 g) butter or margarine	

Preheat the oven to 375°F (190°C, gas mark 5). Grease a 2 pint (1 litre) ovenproof casserole dish with a little oil. Simmer the carrots and celery in a pan of boiling water until only just tender. Drain well and rinse under cold water. Drain again. Combine the pasta and vegetables and layer half the mixture in the base of the casserole dish. Cover with the tomato slices, reserving three slices for use as a garnish. Cover with remaining vegetables and pasta mixture. Melt the butter or margarine in a small, heavy saucepan, stir in the flour and cook for 1 minute. Slowly stir in the milk and bring to the boil. Stir continuously until the sauce just boils and thickens. Add the salt and cayenne pepper to taste and stir in the mustard and most of the cheese. Pour the sauce over the pasta and vegetables. Sprinkle over the remaining cheese and bake in the preheated oven for 30 minutes. Serve garnished with reserved tomato slices and celery leaves.

Variation
This dish is also good with leeks and parsnips instead of carrots and celery. The Cheddar cheese may be replaced with Red Leicester.

VEGETARIAN LASAGNE WITH CHEESE TOPPING
Serves 6

This is a dish to serve to friends who think a meal without meat cannot be exciting.

1 small aubergine, roughly chopped	pinch of brown sugar
1 tablespoon (15 ml) vegetable oil	salt and black pepper
1 small onion, finely chopped	12 oz (350 g) ricotta cheese
8 oz (225 g) mushrooms, sliced	1 egg
8 oz (225 g) tinned tomatoes, coarsely chopped	8 oz (225 g) wholewheat lasagne, cooked and drained
2 tablespoons (30 ml) tomato purée	6 oz (175 g) mozzarella cheese, grated
½ teaspoon dried basil	2 oz (50 g) Parmesan cheese
1 teaspoon dried oregano	

Place the chopped aubergine in a sieve or colander, sprinkle well with salt, cover and leave to drain for 30 minutes. Rinse well.

Heat the oil in a saucepan, add the onion and cook over a moderate heat until soft. Add the aubergine and mushrooms and cook for a further 5 minutes. Add the tomatoes, tomato purée, basil, oregano and brown sugar, stir, cover and simmer for 30 minutes or until thick. Season with salt and black pepper.

Preheat the oven to 350°F (180°C, gas mark 4). In a bowl, combine the ricotta cheese and egg, and mix well. Spread a third of the aubergine sauce over the base of a baking dish, cover with half the lasagne, then spread the ricotta cheese mixture over. Continue layering, first with half the mozzarella cheese, then the second third of the aubergine sauce, then the remaining lasagne, then the remaining aubergine sauce and, finally, the remaining mozzarella. Sprinkle with Parmesan cheese. Bake in the preheated oven for 25-30 minutes, or until the cheese is golden. Serve immediately.

BEANS AND PASTA IN TOMATO SAUCE
Serves 4

This makes an excellent, hearty, main meal with the protein-rich combination of beans and pasta.

½ pint (300 ml) TOMATO SAUCE (see page 199)

1 lb (450 g) tinned white haricot beans

6 oz (175 g) small elbow or shell pasta

1 tablespoon (15 ml) olive oil

1 teaspoon prepared mustard

2 tablespoons (30 ml) fresh parsley, finely chopped

salt and black pepper to taste

2 tablespoons (30 ml) dry roasted cumin seeds, to garnish

Prepare the tomato sauce and keep it hot. Heat the beans in their liquid. Cook the pasta in lots of water until it is *al dente* (just firm to the bite). Pour the pasta into a colander and drain. Drain off the beans and combine with the pasta, olive oil, mustard, tomato sauce and parsley. Season to taste with salt and black pepper and serve garnished with cumin seeds.

SOFT FRIED NOODLES   *Serves 4*

In this Japanese dish, cooked noodles are stir-fried with vegetables and ginger. If available, use buckwheat noodles.

12 oz (350 g) noodles (preferably buckwheat noodles)	½ medium carrot, peeled and grated
4 tablespoons (60 ml) vegetable oil	4 oz (100 g) Chinese cabbage, shredded
1 clove garlic, crushed	1 medium green pepper, cored, seeded and diced
1 tablespoon (15 ml) grated ginger root	black pepper and soya sauce to taste

Cook the noodles in plenty of boiling water until *al dente* (just firm to the bite). Drain them and rinse under lots of cold water. Drain them again and stir into them 1 tablespoon (15 ml) of the oil. Heat the remaining oil in a large frying pan or wok and sauté the garlic and ginger for 2-3 minutes. Add the carrot, cabbage and pepper and sauté until they are just softened. Stir in the noodles and heat through with constant stirring. Season to taste with soya sauce and black pepper and serve.

SPAGHETTI WITH BROWN LENTIL BOLOGNESE SAUCE   *Serves 4*

8 oz (225 g) brown lentils	2 medium carrots, chopped
1 pint (550 ml) water	2 sticks of celery, sliced
1 bay leaf	1 tablespoon (15 ml) tomato purée
sea salt and freshly ground black pepper	16 fl oz (450 ml) vegetable stock (use a stock cube or see page 70)
4 tablespoons (60 ml) olive oil	
2 medium onions, chopped	5 fl oz (150 ml) cider
1 clove garlic, finely chopped	

4 oz (100 g) mushrooms, sliced

1 medium cooking apple, grated

3 tablespoons (45 ml) chopped
  parsley

1 lb (450 g) wholewheat or plain
  spaghetti

Boil the lentils in the water with the bayleaf and seasoning until cooked (about 1 hour). Add more water to the pan as necessary. Heat the olive oil in a large heavy-bottomed saucepan and cook the onions and garlic until soft. Stir in the carrots and celery and continue cooking until the onions are brown. Add the tomato purée, stock and cider. Bring the mixture to the boil and then add the mushrooms and apple. Cover and simmer the sauce for 45 minutes. Add the chopped parsley and more seasoning if necessary. Cook the spaghetti in plenty of boiling salted water until *al dente* (just firm to the bite), adding a little oil to prevent it sticking. Serve either on hot individual plates or on one large serving dish with the lentil sauce piled in the middle.

FRIED NOODLES WITH BROCCOLI
Serves 4

8 oz (225 g) egg noodles

3 tablespoons (45 ml) oil

1 medium onion, diced

2 cloves garlic, crushed

1 in (2.5 cm) piece root ginger,
  finely chopped

12 oz (350 g) broccoli, chopped

3 sticks celery, chopped

dark soya sauce to taste

4 spring onions, chopped

salt and black pepper to taste

fresh parsley, finely chopped

Drop the noodles into lots of boiling salted water and cook them until they are just tender. Drain them and immediately toss them in 1 tablespoon (15 ml) oil, then set them aside. Heat the remaining oil in a large, heavy frying pan or wok and fry the onion, garlic and ginger until the onion is softened. Add the broccoli and celery and stir-fry for 2-3 minutes. Stir in the noodles, then stir-fry over a low heat for a further 2–3 minutes. Add the soya sauce and spring onions, season to taste with salt and pepper and stir-fry for another 1–2 minutes. Serve in individual bowls or in one large tureen, garnished with the parsley.

Variation
Vegetables such as carrots, beansprouts, Chinese cabbage, mushrooms and so on may be substituted for the broccoli and celery.

ROMANA PASTA   *Serves 4-6*

This Italian peasant dish uses the pasta cooking water to moisten the served spaghetti. It is simple, quick and effective.

1 lb (450 g) wholewheat or plain
    spaghetti

6 oz (175 g) Pecorino Romano or
    mature Cheddar cheese

freshly ground black pepper to
    taste

Bring 6–7 pints (3½–4 litres) salted water to the boil. Add the spaghetti and cook until *al dente* (just firm to the bite), stirring occasionally to make sure it doesn't stick together. Put the cheese and black pepper into a serving bowl large enough to hold the cooked spaghetti. Just before the pasta is drained, scoop out a cupful of the cooking water and stir into the cheese and black pepper. Drain the pasta and stir it into the bowl. Add salt to taste if necessary. Serve immediately.

EGG NOODLES IN VEGETABLE STOCK

Serves 4

This quick and filling dish makes a speedy lunchtime meal.

2 tablespoons (30 ml) oil	1-2 fresh or dried red chillies, finely chopped (optional)
1 small onion, sliced	
2 cloves garlic, crushed	3 oz (75 g) beansprouts, washed
2 pints (1 litre) vegetable stock (use stock cubes or see page 70)	4 spring onions, chopped
	12 oz (350 g) egg noodles
1 in (2.5 cm) piece of root ginger, finely chopped	dark soya sauce to taste
salt and black pepper to taste	sliced hard boiled eggs, or thin strips of omelette, or tomato wedges, or chopped celery tops, or fried onion flakes or rings, to garnish
4 oz (100 g) cabbage leaves, shredded	

Heat the oil in a large saucepan and add the onion and garlic. Stir-fry until the onion is softened. Add the stock, ginger and salt and black pepper to taste. Bring the mixture to the boil, reduce the heat, cover and simmer for 15 minutes. Add the cabbage leaves and chillies (if used), increase the heat and bring the mixture to a gentle boil. Add the beansprouts, spring onions and noodles. Loosen the strands of the noodles with a fork and stir in soya sauce to taste. Adjust the seasoning and simmer the soup, covered, for 5-7 minutes or until the noodles are cooked. Transfer the contents of the pan to a serving dish and garnish before serving.

BEANS AND BEANCURD

LENTIL CAYENNE
Serves 4

This is a colourful hotchpotch of browns, reds and greens, spiked with cayenne pepper. Serve with bread or rice or other grains.

1 lb (450 g) brown lentils (for quicker cooking pre-soak for 2-3 hours)

2 tablespoons (30 ml) olive oil

2 cloves garlic, crushed

2 medium onions, chopped

8 oz (225 g) tinned tomatoes, drained, chopped

2 medium green peppers, seeded and chopped

1 teaspoon paprika

1 teaspoon cayenne (more or less for hotter or cooler)

salt and black pepper to taste

2-3 tablespoons (30-45 ml) fresh parsley or mint, finely chopped

Put the lentils in a pan and just cover with water. Cook, covered, until just tender. Add more water as needed, but aim to end the cooking period with the lentils just moist, not sloppy. Heat the oil in another pan and gently brown the garlic and onion. Add the tomatoes, green pepper, paprika and cayenne, stir well and cook for 2-3 minutes. Add the cooked lentils, stir well, season to taste with salt and black pepper, cover the pan and simmer over a very low light for 10 minutes. Remove from the heat, stir in the fresh parsley or mint and serve.

KIDNEY BEAN AND CIDER CASSEROLE

Serves 4

2 tablespoons (30 ml) vegetable oil	2 tablespoons (30 ml) tomato purée
2 cloves garlic, crushed	8 oz (225 g) cooked kidney beans, drained (see pages 26 and 29)
2 medium onions, sliced	
1 medium green pepper, diced	
2 medium courgettes, sliced	salt and black pepper to taste
1 bay leaf	8 fl oz (225 ml) dry cider

Preheat the oven to 375°F (190°C, gas mark 5). Heat the oil in a heavy frying pan and sauté the garlic and onion until golden. Add the green pepper and courgettes, stir and gently sauté until softened. Pour the mixture into a casserole dish and add the remaining ingredients. Mix well, cover and bake in the preheated oven for 40 minutes.

CHILLI BEANS

Serves 6

This is a mild chilli con carne without the meat. Serve with grated cheese sprinkled over the top.

1 tablespoon (15 ml) vegetable oil	½ teaspoon dried oregano
1 small onion, chopped	½ teaspoon dried basil
2 cloves garlic, crushed	½ teaspoon ground coriander
1 dried chilli, seeded and finely chopped or 1-2 teaspoons chilli sauce	salt and black pepper
	1½ lb (700 g) cooked kidney beans, drained (see pages 26 and 29)
14 oz (400 g) canned tomatoes, drained and chopped	
½ teaspoon honey	2 tablespoons (30 ml) cracked wheat
½ teaspoon ground cumin	4 fl oz (100 ml) water

Heat the oil in a saucepan, add the onions, garlic and chilli. Cook until soft, then add the tomatoes, honey, cumin, oregano, basil, coriander and season with salt and pepper. Cook gently for 5 minutes. Add the beans, cracked wheat and water. Bring to the boil, cover and simmer for 30–45 minutes or until thick, stirring occasionally.

HARICOT BEAN GOULASH   *Serves 4-6*

Serve this rich tasting goulash with spaghetti or noodles or bread and a green salad.

4 tablespoons (60 ml) vegetable oil	16 fl oz (450 ml) water or vegetable stock, boiling
1 clove garlic, crushed	2 teaspoons paprika
2 medium onions, thinly sliced	½ teaspoon dry English mustard
8 oz (225 g) mushrooms, sliced	pinch cayenne
1 tablespoon (15 ml) tomato purée	1 teaspoon caraway seeds
	1 bay leaf
1 lb (450 g) haricot beans, soaked overnight, drained	salt and black pepper to taste

Preheat the oven to 325°F (170°C, gas mark 3). Heat the oil in a heavy casserole dish, add the garlic and the onions and sauté until golden. Add the remaining ingredients, except for the salt, and mix well. Cover, bring to the boil and transfer to the oven. Bake for 2–3 hours or until the beans are tender. Salt to taste and serve.

HONEY BAKED BEANS   *Serves 4-6*

Honey baked beans are a distinct improvement on ordinary tinned baked beans. Serve them with wholemeal bread and a green salad for a nutritious and filling meal. They are also good on their own on toast.

1 lb (450 g) haricot beans, soaked overnight and drained	4 tablespoons (60 ml) tomato purée
2 tablespoons (30 ml) vegetable oil	1 tablespoon (15 ml) French mustard (or other mild mustard)
2 medium onions, chopped	
3 tablespoons (45 ml) honey	salt to taste

Place the beans covered with water in a large pan, bring to the boil, lower the heat and simmer until tender (about 1½ hours). Drain and reserve the liquid. Preheat the oven to 350°F (180°C, gas mark 4). In a casserole dish (about 9–12 in (23–30 cm) in diameter) heat the oil and sauté the onion until softened. Add the drained beans, 8 fl oz (225 ml) of the cooking liquid and the remaining ingredients. Mix well, cover and cook in the preheated oven for 20 minutes, uncover the dish and cook for a further 20 minutes.

FLAGEOLET BEANS IN RICH TOMATO SAUCE

Serves 4

This is vastly superior to anything you can get in tins, and, if you really want to, you can eat it hot on toast.

175 g (6 oz) dried flageolet beans, soaked overnight, drained	1 clove garlic, well crushed
250 ml (8 fl oz) TOMATO SAUCE (see page 199)	5 ml (1 teaspoon) dried oregano
½ bunch spring onions, washed, trimmed of coarse green leaves, finely sliced	15 ml (1 tablespoon) chopped parsley
	few leaves of fresh thyme
	salt and pepper to taste

Cook the beans in fresh unsalted water until tender (about 1–1½ hours). Drain, then combine them with the tomato sauce, onions and garlic. Add the herbs and the seasonings and set aside to cool. Retest the seasonings when the salad is cold.

CHICKPEAS SPANISH STYLE   *Serves 4*

This is a chilli-hot casserole of chickpeas, green pepper, garlic and tomatoes.

1 lb (450 g) chickpeas, soaked overnight, drained	1 lb (450 g) fresh or tinned tomatoes, chopped
2 pints (1.1 litres) water	½-1 dried or fresh chilli, finely chopped or ½-1 teaspoon hot pepper sauce
3 tablespoons (45 ml) vegetable oil (olive oil if possible)	
1 medium onion, diced	1 tablespoon (15 ml) fresh parsley, chopped
3 cloves garlic, crushed	salt to taste
1 medium green pepper, chopped	

Put the chickpeas, water and 1 tablespoon (15 ml) oil in a large saucepan and bring to the boil, cover, reduce heat and set to simmer. Meanwhile sauté the onion and garlic until golden in the remaining oil in a frying pan. Add the green pepper and cook until soft. Add the remaining ingredients to the frying pan, stir well, and gently simmer the mixture for 20–30 minutes. As the chickpeas approach tenderness (after about 1 hour), add this tomato sauce to them and continue cooking until the chickpeas are tender. Serve.

VIRGINIA BLACK-EYED BEANS   *Serves 4*

This is a very simple but tasty bean dish.

1 lb (450 g) black-eyed beans, soaked overnight and drained	2 whole cloves
	¼ teaspoon black pepper
1 medium onion, quartered	water
½ teaspoon dried thyme	salt to taste
1 bay leaf	

Put the beans, onion, thyme, bay leaf, cloves and black pepper into a heavy saucepan. Just cover with water and bring to the boil. Cover, reduce the heat and simmer for 1-1½ hours or until the beans are very tender. Season to taste with salt and serve. During the cooking time, check occasionally and add water as required.

THAI CURRIED BEANCURD WITH VEGETABLES

Serves 4

The vegetables given in this recipe are only suggestions and any suitable combination you have available may be used. This curry, unlike most Thai curries, does not use coconut milk and it is a little quicker and simpler to prepare than usual. Serve with rice.

3 tablespoons (45 ml) vegetable oil	4 oz (100 g) cauliflower, cut into florets
2 teaspoons curry powder	4 oz (100 g) cabbage or Chinese cabbage, coarsely shredded
8 oz (225 g) beancurd (see page 31), cut into 1 in (2.5 cm) cubes	4 oz (100 g) fresh mushrooms, sliced
1 teaspoon grated lemon rind or chopped lemon grass	2 tablespoons (30 ml) soya sauce
	2 teaspoons sugar
4 oz (100 g) green beans, cut into 2 in (5 cm) lengths	finely chopped coriander, mint or parsley leaves to garnish

Heat the oil in a large pan or wok and stir-fry the curry powder for 1-2 minutes. Add the beancurd and lemon rind and continue to stir-fry for a further 6-7 minutes. Add the green beans, cauliflower, cabbage, mushrooms and soya sauce. Cook, stirring, until the vegetables are tender enough to eat but still retain some 'bite' (about 4-5 minutes). Stir in the sugar and serve garnished with mint, coriander or parsley leaves.

TOFU (BEANCURD) BURGERS   *Serves 4*

These are delicious, low-fat burgers.

4 tablespoons (60 ml) vegetable oil	2 tablespoons (30 ml) wholemeal flour
½ medium onion, finely diced	1 egg, beaten
1 small green pepper, cored, seeded and finely diced	4 oz (100 g) cheese, grated
1 medium carrot, grated	salt to taste
12 oz (350 g) tofu (beancurd – see page 31) drained	wholemeal flour for dusting

Heat half the oil in the frying pan and add the onions, pepper and carrot. Stir-fry until the onion is softened. Mash the beancurd in a mixing bowl and add the fried vegetables, flour, eggs, cheese and salt. Mix well and then, with wet hands, form the mixture into about 12 small burger shapes. Dust them with flour and fry them brown on both sides in the remaining oil.

BEANCURD AND FRIED RICE   *Serves 4*

Note that for fried rice dishes it is best to use cold cooked, rather than freshly, cooked rice. Once cooked rice has cooled, much of its moisture has evaporated and this allows the frying oil to more easily coat the grains and thus stop them sticking to each other.

2 tablespoons (30 ml) oil	1 lb (450 g) cooked rice (see pages 24 and 25)
1 clove garlic, crushed	6 oz (175 g) beancurd (see page 31) cut into 1 in (2.5 cm) cubes
1 medium onion, diced	
4 oz (100 g) mushrooms, sliced	
4 oz (100 g) celery or French beans, chopped	1 egg
	2 tablespoons (30 ml) soya sauce

Heat the oil in a heavy frying pan. Add the crushed garlic and onion. Sauté until the onions are just soft, and then add the mushrooms and celery or French beans. Fry gently for 2–3 minutes. Stir in the rice and beancurd. Heat through, stirring constantly. Break the egg over the mixture, sprinkle on the soya sauce and mix well. Serve immediately.

Note: For fried rice with a less creamy texture, replace the egg with strips of omelette.

RED COOKED BEANCURD
AND CUCUMBER   *Serves 4*

This is a summer dish (or a winter side dish to add some colour and freshness to a starchy meal), served chilled with perhaps cold noodles or a rice salad.

1 medium cucumber, seeded, cut into strips 2 in (5 cm) long and ¼ in (5 mm) thick	2 tablespoons (30 ml) soya sauce
salt	1 red pepper, seeded, cut into strips 2 in (5 cm) long and ¼ in (5 mm) thick
8 oz (225 g) beancurd (see page 31), cut into 1 in (2.5 cm) cubes	2 teaspoons grated fresh ginger root
4 tablespoons (60 ml) vegetable oil (sesame seed oil for preference)	4 tablespoons (60 ml) rice or cider vinegar
	2 teaspoons sugar

Place the cucumber in a colander and sprinkle liberally with salt. Leave to stand for 20 minutes. Fry the beancurd in half the oil in a wok or frying pan and gently brown all sides of the cubes. Remove the beancurd from the pan and put into a bowl, sprinkle over the soya sauce and leave to marinate. Rinse the cucumber under cold running water, drain and pat dry on a tea towel. Add the remaining oil to the wok or pan and add the cucumber, red pepper and ginger. Stir-fry over a high heat for 2–3 minutes. Transfer the contents of the pan to a serving dish. Add the vinegar, sugar, beancurd and soya sauce. Gently mix together and leave to marinate in the refrigerator for 4 or more hours. It will keep for up to 3 days in the refrigerator.

SOYA BEAN, GINGER AND POTATO LAYERS   *Serves 4*

This is only a convenient dish to make if you already have a reserve of cooked soya beans. If not, substitute tinned beans such as chickpeas, red beans or broad beans.

1 tablespoon (15 ml) vegetable oil	1 stick celery, chopped finely
12 oz (350 g) tomatoes, sliced	1 in (2.5 cm) piece stem ginger, peeled and chopped
12 oz (350 g) soya beans, cooked (see pages 26 and 29)	1 lb (450 g) potatoes, peeled and sliced
1 small onion, grated or chopped finely	3 tablespoons (45 ml) soya sauce
1 clove garlic, crushed	1 oz (25 g) vegetable margarine

Preheat the oven to 375°F (190°C, gas mark 5). Oil a casserole dish and put half of the tomatoes in the bottom, then a layer of some of the soya beans. Mix the onion, garlic, celery and ginger together and spread some of this mixture evenly over the beans. Cover with a layer of potato slices. Keep layering in this way, finishing with the potatoes. Sprinkle the soya sauce over, dot with margarine and bake in the preheated oven for 45 minutes, covered. Uncover and continue baking for another 45 minutes. Serve.

RICH BEAN, VEGETABLE AND CHESTNUT HOTPOT   *Serves 4*

The chestnuts impart a rich flavour to this cornucopia of vegetables and beans.

1 large onion, chopped	3 tablespoons (45 ml) vegetable oil
2 teaspoons fresh chopped mixed herbs or 1 teaspoon dried herbs	1 large carrot, scrubbed and chopped
1 bay leaf	1 stick celery, chopped

¼ each of medium turnip and swede, diced

½ medium parsnip, diced

2 oz (50 g) fresh broad beans (optional)

1 green pepper, seeded and chopped

4 oz (100 g) cauliflower florets

2 oz (50 g) mushrooms

8 oz (225 g) tomatoes, skinned, chopped

1 tablespoon (15 ml) tomato purée

12 oz (350 g) single type of bean or mixed beans, soaked overnight

2 oz (50 g) dried chestnuts, soaked overnight, drained and halved

1 clove garlic

2 tablespoons (30 ml) soya sauce

2 tablespoons (30 ml) chopped parsley

salt to taste

Sauté the onions, herbs and bay leaf in the oil in a large saucepan. After 5 minutes add the carrot, celery, turnip, swede, parsnip, broad beans (if using), pepper, cauliflower and mushrooms. Cover and cook gently for 10 minutes, stirring occasionally. Stir in the tomatoes, tomato purée, soaked beans and chestnuts and just cover with water. Bring to the boil, cover the pan, lower the heat and simmer for 1 hour or until the beans are cooked. Uncover the pan, ladle some hot juice into a blender and add the garlic, soya sauce and parsley. Liquidize for 2 minutes and pour back into the stew. Season to taste with salt and serve.

Note: This stew may be cooked in a pressure cooker. In this case, put the lid on the cooker after adding the tomatoes, tomato purée, beans, chestnuts and water, bring up to pressure and cook for 25 minutes. Depressurize, then follow recipe as above.

BEAN PIE

Serves 4

Any kind of bean can be used for this tasty dish but cannellini beans prove ideal for this combination of beans, vegetables and crisp topping.

2 onions, chopped	1 × 14 oz (400 g) tin tomatoes, roughly chopped
1 green pepper, chopped	
oil (preferably olive oil)	TOPPING
1 tablespoon (15 ml) tomato purée	4 oz (100 g) grated cheese
1 tablespoon (15 ml) brown sugar	1 egg, beaten
1 teaspoon dried oregano	8 oz (225 g) cottage cheese
salt and black pepper to taste	salt and black pepper to taste
14 oz (400 g) tin cannellini beans	

Preheat oven to 350°-375°F (180°-190°C, gas mark 4–5). Fry the onion and green pepper in a little oil for 2–3 minutes. Add tomatoes, tomato purée, sugar and oregano. Season well and simmer until the vegetables are quite soft. Strain the beans and reserve the liquid. Combine the beans with the vegetable mixture in a 2 pint (generous 1 litre) casserole. If necessary, to ensure all the beans are covered, add some of the drained bean juice. Mix the topping ingredients together and spread over the mixture in the casserole. Bake for 30 minutes in the preheated oven, until golden brown and bubbling.

CHICKPEA, BUTTERBEAN AND TAHINI CASSEROLE

Serves 4

This casserole is simple to prepare and very tasty and nutritious.

2 medium onions, chopped	2 tablespoons (30 ml) vegetable oil
2 cloves garlic, crushed	1 tablespoon tahini

8 oz (225 g) chickpeas, soaked and cooked (see pages 26 and 28) or 1 lb (450 g) tinned chickpeas, drained

4 oz (100 g) butterbeans, soaked and cooked (see pages 26 and 28) or 8 oz (225 g) tinned butterbeans, drained

1 lb (450 g) tomatoes, skinned, chopped

¼ teaspoon grated nutmeg

2 teaspoons chopped fresh basil or 1 teaspoon dried basil

sea salt to taste

Preheat the oven to 350°F (180°C, gas mark 4). Sauté the onions and garlic gently in the oil in a frying pan for 5 minutes. Put them in a casserole dish with the tahini, chickpeas, butterbeans, tomatoes, nutmeg, basil, salt to taste, and mix well. Cover and cook for 45 minutes in the hot oven.

CHICKPEA AND VEGETABLE CURRY

Serves 6

Serve this delicious thick, spicy curry with rice, chapattis and chutney.

2 tablespoons (30 ml) vegetable oil

1 large onion, chopped

2 cloves garlic, crushed

2 teaspoons (10 ml) ground cardamom

1 teaspoon (5 ml) ground cumin

½ teaspoon (2.5 ml) chilli powder or hot pepper sauce

2 teaspoons (10 ml) ground turmeric

8 oz (225 g) carrots, sliced

4 sticks celery, sliced

1 in (2.5 cm) piece fresh ginger root, grated or 1 teaspoon (5 ml) ground ginger

5 fl oz (150 ml) vegetable stock or water

5 fl oz (150 ml) natural low-fat yoghurt

salt and black pepper

4 oz (100 g) button mushrooms, rinsed

12 oz (350 g) cooked chickpeas (see pages 26 and 28), drained

2 oz (50 g) desiccated coconut, lightly toasted until golden

Melt the oil in a saucepan, add the onion and garlic and cook until soft. Add the cardamom, cumin, chilli and turmeric and cook, stirring continuously, for 5 minutes. Add the carrots and celery and mix well. Stir in the ginger, stock and yoghurt. Season to taste with salt and black pepper, bring to a very low simmer, cover and cook gently for 30 minutes. Add the mushrooms and chickpeas and continue cooking for 10 minutes. Sprinkle the coconut over the dish and serve.

BUTTERBEANS TOPPED WITH BASIL AND TOMATO SAUCE   *Serves 4*

½ lb (225 g) butterbeans, soaked overnight

2 medium onions, chopped

1 large clove garlic, finely chopped

2 teaspoons chopped fresh basil or 1 teaspoon dried basil

3 tablespoons (45 ml) vegetable oil

14 oz (400 g) canned tomatoes, drained and chopped (reserve juice)

1 tablespoon (15 ml) tomato ketchup

2 teaspoons miso (see page 30)

soya sauce to taste

fresh parsley, chopped, to garnish

Drain the butterbeans, cover them with fresh water and boil, covered, until they are just soft (about 1½ hours). Meanwhile, sauté the onions, garlic and basil in the oil in a large pan. Add the tomatoes, ketchup and juice from the tomatoes and bring to a low boil. Mix the miso to a paste with some of the hot liquid from the pan and stir in. Add soya sauce to taste. Combine the beans, drained, with the sauce, top with lots of chopped parsley and serve.

LENTILS AND SPINACH

Serves 4

8 oz (225 g) lentils, soaked and drained

1 lb (450 g) spinach, washed and chopped

1 medium onion, finely chopped

2 cloves garlic, crushed

2 oz (50 g) butter

½ teaspoon ground cumin

½ teaspoon ground coriander

salt and black pepper to taste

juice of 1 lemon

2 hard-boiled eggs, peeled and sliced

Cover the lentils in water and cook until tender. Cook the spinach until tender in a little water. Drain the lentils and spinach and combine together. Fry the onion and garlic golden brown in the butter in a large frying pan and stir in the cumin, coriander, and salt and black pepper to taste. Fry a further 2 minutes and then stir in the lentil and spinach mixture. Add the lemon juice and heat through, stirring. Adjust the seasoning and serve garnished with the slices of hard-boiled egg. This dish is also good cold.

GREEN LENTIL AND WHOLEWHEAT LASAGNE

Serves 4

This low-fat dish is moist and tasty and enjoyed by vegans, vegetarians and demi-vegetarians alike.

1 large onion, chopped

3 cloves garlic, crushed

2 tablespoons (30 ml) vegetable oil

8 oz (225 g) green lentils

12 oz (350 g) canned tomatoes, drained and chopped (reserve juice)

1 pint (0.5 litre) water or stock (use juice from tomatoes as part of this)

1 teaspoon garam masala

salt to taste

6 oz (175 g) wholewheat lasagne, cooked and drained

4 oz (100 g) hazelnuts, roasted or ground

Sauté the onion and garlic in the oil in a saucepan for 10 minutes. Stir in the lentils and tomatoes and pour in the water or stock. Bring to the boil, cover and simmer for 45 minutes. Mix in the garam masala and sea salt to taste. Remove from the heat. Strain off the liquid and reserve. Preheat the oven to 400°F (200°C, gas mark 6). Using a greased shallow baking dish, and starting and finishing with the lentil mixture, layer the lasagne with the lentils. Pour over the reserved liquid. Top with the ground hazelnuts and bake for 45 minutes in the hot oven. Serve immediately.

BARLEY AND LENTIL PATTIES   *Serves 6*

8 oz (225 g) whole barley	½ teaspoon freshly ground black pepper
4 oz (100 g) red lentils	1½ oz (40 g) wholemeal flour
5 oz (150 g) grated Cheddar cheese	1 tablespoon (15 ml) finely chopped parsley
1 small egg, beaten	sunflower seed oil for shallow frying
2 tablespoons (30 ml) tomato purée	
½ teaspoon salt	

Cook the barley in plenty of water until tender (allow up to ¾ hour for this). Cook the lentils separately in at least twice their volume of water. Drain both the barley and lentils and combine them with all the other ingredients except for the oil. Mix well and form into patties approximately ½ in (1.25 cm) thick. Shallow fry the patties until golden brown on both sides in hot sunflower seed oil. Serve hot with a good homemade hot tomato sauce (see page 199).

LENTILS AND NOODLES IN BUTTER
Serves 4

Pasta, perhaps brought back from Italy many centuries ago, is normally used in Arab cooking in conjunction with rice or lentils or both. Like the Chinese, some Arabs eat noodles on New Year's Eve when the long noodles become symbols of hoped-for longevity.

8 oz (225 g) brown lentils	2 medium onions, finely diced
salt and black pepper to taste	½ teaspoon coriander
8 oz (225 g) thin noodles	¼-½ teaspoon cayenne
4 oz (100 g) butter	1 teaspoon dried basil

Wash and drain the lentils and put them in a heavy-based pan. Cover with water, add salt to taste and bring to the boil. Reduce the heat, cover and simmer for 1 hour or until the lentils are just tender. Drain and set the lentils aside (reserve the cooking liquid for stock). Meanwhile put the noodles in a large pan of salted boiling water and cook, stirring, until just tender. Drain and reserve. In a large heavy frying pan, melt half the butter and fry the onions until softened and lightly browned. Stir in the spices and basil and cook a further 2 minutes. Mix in the cooked lentils and noodles, season to taste with salt and black pepper and heat through. Melt the remaining butter, pour over the food and serve, either as a side dish or a light main dish.

RED BEAN ENCHILADES

Serves 6

Enchilades are tortillas, the Mexican corn meal pancakes, stuffed with a bean, vegetable or cheese filling and baked with a sauce and cheese. Tortillas are not difficult to make but obtaining the right ingredients for an authentic flavour is not always easy, so do substitute shop bought tortillas for those given in the recipe if you wish.

TORTILLAS

2 tablespoons (30 ml) vegetable
   margarine

12 fl oz (350 ml) water, boiling

4½ oz (125 g) cornmeal
   (stoneground if possible)

or 12 shop-bought tortillas

5 oz (150 g) wholemeal flour

FILLING

2 tablespoons (30 ml) vegetable
   oil

½ teaspoon ground cumin

1 onion, finely diced

½ teaspoon chilli powder (more
   or less may be used

1 green pepper, seeded, finely
   chopped

   depending on how hot you like
   it)

2 tablespoons (30 ml) finely
   chopped parsley

½ pt (275 ml) TOMATO SAUCE
   (see page 199)

1 lb (450 g) cooked red kidney
   beans, drained

salt to taste

TOPPING

1¼ pints (750 ml) TOMATO
   SAUCE (see page 199)

4 oz (100 g) Cheddar cheese,
   grated

To make the tortillas, stir the margarine into the boiling water in a mixing bowl and then stir in the cornmeal. Set this aside to cool to room temperature and then mix in the flour. Knead this dough for a few minutes, adding more water if it is too stiff and more flour if it is too soft. Now divide the dough into 12 portions and roll each into a ball. Flatten each ball on a lightly floured board and roll it out to about a 6 in (15 cm) diameter circle. Flour the rolling pin and board as necessary to stop the dough sticking. Stack the tortillas as you make them and cover them with a damp cloth. Heat an 8 in (20 cm) ungreased non-stick frying pan or plain heavy frying pan over a medium to high flame and cook the tortillas one at a time for about 1 minute (until lightly flecked brown) on each side. Stack them and cover with a cloth to keep them warm and pliable. If they are not to be used immediately, they can be softened before filling by heating them for a few seconds on each side in a hot frying pan.

Now prepare the filling. Heat the oil in a saucepan and sauté the onions for 2 minutes. Add the green pepper and parsley and sauté for a further 2 minutes. Add the kidney beans, cumin, chilli powder, tomato sauce and salt to taste. Bring the mixture to the boil, cover, reduce heat and simmer for 5 minutes. Remove from the heat and put the filling on one side.

Preheat the oven to 350°F (180°C, gas mark 4). Grease a large baking dish. Put 2-3 tablespoons (30-40 ml) of filling onto each tortilla roll them up, and place the filled tortillas seam-side down, side by side in the prepared baking dish. Pour over the tomato sauce for topping and sprinkle the cheese over the top. Bake in the preheated oven for 30 minutes or until the cheese starts to brown and the sauce bubbles. Serve immediately.

DRESSINGS AND SAUCES

BEANCURD DRESSING

Makes about 8 fl oz

This vegan dressing has the consistency of mayonnaise.

6 oz (175 g) fresh beancurd (see page 31), drained

1 tablespoon (15 ml) onion, chopped

1 tablespoon (15 ml) olive oil or other vegetable oil

1 tablespoon (15 ml) water

1 teaspoon lemon juice

1 teaspoon honey

salt to taste

Place all the ingredients in a liquidizer or food processor. Blend together at high speed. Adjust the seasoning.

JAPANESE MUSTARD DRESSING

Makes 4-5 tablespoons (60-75 ml)

1 teaspoon prepared English mustard (or wasabi)

2 tablespoons (30 ml) rice or cider vinegar

1 tablespoon (30 ml) soya sauce

1-2 teaspoons sugar

Combine the mustard, vinegar and soya sauce in a small mixing bowl, add sugar to taste and stir well to dissolve the sugar.

BASIC MAYONNAISE   *Makes about ½ pt (300 ml)*

1 large egg	lemon juice or wine vinegar (up to 2 tablespoons (30 ml)) to taste
1 teaspoon prepared mustard	
good pinch of salt	additional salt, black pepper, paprika or cayenne to taste
9 fl oz (250 ml) vegetable oil	

Break the egg into a bowl or liquidizer goblet and add the mustard and salt. Beat or blend at medium speed until the mixture thickens slightly. Still beating or blending, pour in the oil from a measuring jug, drop by drop initially and then, as it begins to thicken, in a slow but steady stream until all the oil is absorbed. Carefully beat or blend in the lemon juice or wine vinegar and season to taste with additional salt, pepper, paprika or cayenne. Store in a cool place. Mayonnaise will keep for not much longer than a day.

BASIC VINAIGRETTE DRESSING   *Makes 6 fl oz (175 ml)*

4½ fl oz (120 ml) vegetable oil	salt and pepper to taste
2 tablespoons (30 ml) wine vinegar, cider vinegar or lemon juice	1 teaspoon prepared mustard (optional)

Place all the ingredients in a bowl or liquidizer and beat or blend well. Test and adjust seasoning if necessary.

BASIC FRENCH DRESSING

Makes 7 fl oz (200 ml)

¼ pint (150 ml) olive oil

¾ teaspoon salt

pinch freshly ground black pepper

3 tablespoons cider vinegar or wine vinegar or lemon juice

Shake all the ingredients together in a jar, or whirl in a blender for a few seconds. For variations add all or one of the following: ½ teaspoon dry mustard, ½ teaspoon paprika, 1 crushed clove of garlic, 1 tablespoon minced onion.

GREEN SAUCE

Makes 10 fl oz (300 ml)

This is a good general purpose sauce. You can use it on many hot or cold young, tender vegetables.

1 bunch of good fresh watercress, well washed

1 tablespoon (15 ml) vegetable oil

5 fl oz (150 ml) BASIC MAYONNAISE (see page 195)

4 fl oz (100 ml) yoghurt

salt and pepper to taste

Trim the watercress of its roots and remove any discoloured leaves. Plunge the trimmed watercress into a pan of well-salted boiling water for little more than 10 seconds. This may seem a minor step, but it does greatly enhance the colour of the finished sauce. Drain and refresh the watercress under cold running water until it is quite chilled. Squeeze the watercress free of any excess water, roughly chop it, place it in a liquidizer goblet with the oil and blend it to a smooth purée. Mix the watercress purée, the mayonnaise and the yoghurt together in a small mixing bowl. Season to taste with salt and pepper.

BÉCHAMEL SAUCE   *Makes about 14 fl oz (400 ml)*

1 oz (25 g) butter	bay leaf
2 tablespoons (30 ml) finely diced onion	pinch of nutmeg
1 oz (25 g) wholemeal flour	salt and freshly ground black pepper to taste
10 fl oz (275 ml) milk	

Melt the butter in a heavy saucepan over a low heat. Add the onion and sauté until softened and transparent. Stir in the flour to form a smooth paste and cook, stirring, for 2–3 minutes. Add the milk to the pan slowly, stirring constantly. Continue cooking and stirring until the sauce thickens. Add the bay leaf, nutmeg and salt and black pepper and simmer, covered, over a very low heat for 10 minutes. Stir occasionally.

CHEESE SAUCE   *Makes about 14 fl oz (400 ml)*

1 recipe quantity BÉCHAMEL SAUCE (see above), freshly made	2 oz (50 g) grated Cheddar cheese (or other suitable cheese)
	1 teaspoon prepared English mustard (optional)

As soon as the béchamel sauce is cooked, stir in the grated cheese until it has melted. For extra flavour, add the mustard if desired.

PEANUT SAUCE   *Makes 12 fl oz (350 ml)*

Serve this dressing hot or at room temperature on cooked and uncooked vegetable salads.

1 tablespoon (15 ml) vegetable oil	1 teaspoon brown sugar
1 clove garlic, crushed	1 tablespoon (15 ml) lemon juice
1 small onion, diced	8 fl oz (225 g) water
4 oz (100 g) roasted (unsalted) peanuts or 4 oz (100 g) peanut butter	salt to taste

Lightly brown the garlic and onion in the oil. Transfer the garlic, onion and frying oil to a liquidizer or food processor and add all the other ingredients. Blend to a smooth mixture. Transfer the sauce to a pan, bring to the boil and then simmer over a low heat, stirring, for 5 minutes. Use immediately or allow to cool.

Variation
For a spicy, hot peanut sauce in the South–East Asian style, add 1-2 deseeded, chopped, red chillies to the garlic and onion in the pan.

TAHINI SAUCE   *Makes ½ pint (300 ml)*

This sauce is excellent just on its own with bread, or as a salad dressing. Also serve it with rice and vegetable dishes.

2 cloves garlic, crushed	4 fl oz (100 ml) water
1 teaspoon salt	juice of 2 lemons
4 fl oz (100 ml) tahini	

Mash the garlic with the salt in a bowl. Slowly beat in the tahini, water and lemon juice in that order. Blend well, using an electric blender if you like. For a thicker or thinner sauce use less or more water and lemon juice respectively.

Variation
Add 4 fl oz (100 ml) natural yoghurt to the tahini sauce for a thicker, sharper flavoured taste.

TOMATO SAUCE

Makes about 1½ pt (850 ml)

2 oz (50 g) butter or vegetable oil	2 teaspoons crushed oregano
1 medium onion, finely diced	2 tablespoons (30 ml) fresh parsley, chopped
2 lb (900 g) fresh or tinned tomatoes (drained)	1 bay leaf
4 cloves garlic, crushed	salt and pepper to taste
1 medium green pepper, seeded, cored, diced	

Melt the butter in a heavy saucepan or pour in the oil, and fry the onions over a low heat until soft. Skin fresh tomatoes by dropping them in boiling water for a minute or two, then lift them out and peel off the skin. Alternatively use tinned tomatoes, drained. In either case chop the tomatoes into small pieces and add them, with the garlic and green pepper, to the onions, stir well and simmer for 10 minutes. Add the herbs and season to taste with salt and black pepper. Simmer for a further 10 minutes and allow to cool. Use immediately or store in airtight jars, pouring a thin film of oil over the top of the sauce before screwing on the lid.

Variation
For a thicker tomato sauce, suitable for some types of pizza and the preparation of stuffings for vegetable and pasta dishes, add 6 oz (175 g) tomato purée with the chopped tomatoes.

RAW TOMATO SAUCE   *Makes ½ pt (300 ml)*

Use good, fresh, ripe tomatoes for this sauce.

18 oz (500 g) ripe tomatoes, skinned and seeded	1 tablespoon (15 ml) parsley, finely chopped
1 tablespoon (15 ml) wine vinegar	1 teaspoon dried oregano
2 tablespoons (30 ml) olive oil	salt and black pepper to taste

Place all the ingredients in a liquidizer and blend at low speed until a smooth sauce is obtained. Use the sauce over delicate vegetables, either as it is or thinned with whipping cream.

BREADS AND CAKES

YEASTED BREAD ROLLS
Makes 18

1 oz fresh yeast or 2 level
   teaspoons active dried yeast

approximately 3 fl oz (75 ml)
   warm water

1 tablespoon (15 ml) brown sugar

1 teaspoon salt

1 lb (450 g) strong white flour or
   8 oz (225 g) strong white flour
   and 8 oz (225 g) 100 per cent
   wholemeal flour

2 tablespoons (30 ml) vegetable
   oil or butter

8 fl oz (225 ml) milk

1 egg, beaten

Mix yeast, warm water and sugar into a smooth paste and set aside in a warm place for 15–20 minutes or until the mixture has frothed up. Combine salt, flour, oil and milk in a mixing bowl, add yeast mixture and mix into a fairly soft dough which easily comes away from the sides of the bowl. If necessary add extra water. Turn the dough onto a floured board, cover with a damp cloth and leave to rest for 10 minutes. Now knead for 5 minutes to form a smooth elastic dough. Place in a clean greased bowl, cover with a warm damp cloth and leave to rise in a warm place for 45 minutes to 1 hour.

Preheat oven to 425°F (210°C, gas mark 6). Turn dough onto a floured board, shape into a long cylindrical roll and cut into 18 portions. Shape each into a roll and place them at least 1 in (2.5 cm) apart on a greased baking sheet. Leave to rise for 10–15 minutes, brush the tops with the beaten egg and bake for 15–20 minutes in the preheated oven until nicely browned.

WHOLEMEAL BREAD *Makes 2 × 1lb (450 g) loaves*

This bread keeps well, and it can be used up to one week after baking. All wholemeal flours do not bake in the same way, so do experiment with different brands of flour (and with the given recipe) until the bread you make is exactly to your liking.

2 teaspoons brown sugar	1½ lb (700 g) 100 per cent wholemeal flour
¾ oz (20 g) fresh yeast or 1 level tablespoon (15 ml) active dried yeast	1 tablespoon (15 ml) salt
	1 tablespoon (15 ml) vegetable oil
¾ pint (425 ml) slightly warm water	cracked wheat or sesame seeds (optional)

Mix the sugar, yeast and a little of the water into a smooth paste in a small bowl and set aside in a warm place until the mixture has frothed up (approximately 15 minutes). Put the flour and salt into a large mixing bowl, add the yeast mixture, oil and remaining water. Knead the mixture until you have a smooth springy dough that comes away from the sides of the bowl. Turn the dough onto a floured board and knead well for about 5 minutes (longer if you have strong arms). Wash, dry and slightly grease the mixing bowl, place the dough in it, cover the bowl with a warm damp cloth and set it aside in a warm place for 1-1½ hours or until the dough has risen to double its original size.

Knead the dough again for 5 minutes and then divide it into 2 equal parts. Shape the dough pieces and place them into two lightly buttered 1 lb (450 g) bread tins. If desired, sprinkle the cracked wheat or sesame seeds on the top of each loaf, cover the tins with a warm damp cloth and leave them in a warm place for 30-45 minutes or until the dough has risen to the top of the tins. Preheat the oven to 450°F (230°C, gas mark 8), place the tins in the centre of the oven and bake for 40 minutes. Remove the bread from the oven, tip the loaves out of the tins and knock the underside. If the bread sounds hollow like a drum it is cooked. If the bread does not sound hollow, return the loaves upside down, to the oven and bake for a further 10 minutes at 375°F (190°C, gas mark 5). Leave the bread to cool on a wire rack, or resting across the top of the empty bread tins.

JACK'S GREEK COUNTRY BREAD

Makes 2 × 1½ lb (700 g) loaves

2 tablespoon (30 ml) sugar	2 oz (50 g) vegetable margarine
1 tablespoon (15 ml) active dried yeast	1 teaspoon salt
4 fl oz (100 ml) warm water	2 lbs 4 oz (1 kg) strong white flour
8 fl oz (225 ml) milk	1 tablespoon (15 ml) melted butter or margarine

Put 1 tablespoon (15 ml) of sugar in a jug and sprinkle with the yeast. Add the warm water and allow the yeast mixture to froth up to double its size in a warm place (about 10 minutes). Heat the milk gently in a saucepan and stir in the rest of the sugar, the margarine and the salt. Sift the flour into a mixing bowl. Make a well in the middle and pour in the yeast mixture. Stir with a large knife. Stir in the warm milk mixture, then knead the dough well with the hands. Cover the bowl with a warm damp cloth and place in a warm place to allow the dough to double in size (1-1½ hours). Knead the dough again and then allow it to rise for a further 1-1½ hours. Knead again for a few minutes and break into two equal parts. Shape the dough pieces and place them into two lightly greased 1½ lb (700 g) bread tins or leave round on a greased baking tray. Brush the tops of the loaves with the melted margarine or butter and cover with a cloth. Allow the loaves to rise again for a further 1 hour.

While the loaves are rising, preheat the oven to 375°F (190°C, gas mark 5). When the loaves have risen bake them in the oven until they are golden (about 45 minutes). Cool on a wire rack.

MOROCCAN BREAD *Makes 2 × 1 lb (450 g) loaves*

In Morocco, bread is made from wholemeal flour – it is quite heavy, but nutritious and tasty. Like other Middle Eastern breads, it is baked on flat trays in large, airy ovens. Baking temperatures are quite high and cooking times short.

10 oz (275 g) 100 per cent wholemeal flour	6 fl oz (150 ml) warm milk
10 oz (275 g) strong white flour	2 oz (50 g) melted butter
1 teaspoon salt	1 tablespoon (15 ml) anise or fennel seeds
1 oz (25 g) fresh yeast or 2 teaspoons dried yeast	1½ teaspoons caraway seeds
2 teaspoons sugar	warm water

Combine the flours and salt and mix well. Make a well in the centre. Dissolve the yeast and sugar in the milk and pour into the flour. Add the melted butter, anise or fennel seeds and caraway seeds, and stir in enough warm water to form a firm dough. Knead the dough on a floured board for 5 minutes and then form it into 2 equal-sized round balls. Grease 2 baking sheets and place a ball on each. Roll, or flatten by hand, each ball into a disc of about 8 in (20 cm) diameter. Cover each with a dampened cloth and set them aside in a warm place for 2-3 hours or until the 2 loaves have doubled in size. Preheat the oven to 450°F (230°C, gas mark 7). Bake the bread at this temperature for 10 minutes. Reduce the temperature to 350°F (175°C, gas mark 4) and bake for a further 30 minutes. Remove from the oven and cool on a wire rack.

RYE AND WHEAT BREAD *Makes 3 long loaves*

Rye flour contains less gluten than wheat flour and consequently rises less in the bread-making process. In this recipe we combine rye flour with wheat flour to get a loaf that has both the distinctive taste of rye bread and the lighter texture of wheat bread.

2 lbs (1 kg) 100 per cent wholemeal flour	1 teaspoon honey or molasses
12 oz (350 g) rye flour	1½-1¾ pints (0.8-1 litre) warm water
1 teaspoon salt	2 tablespoons (30 ml) caraway seeds
2 tablespoons (30 ml) vegetable oil	
2 oz (50 g) fresh yeast or 2 tablespoons (30 ml) dried yeast	

In a large bowl mix the wholemeal and rye flours together with the salt, then rub in the oil. Dissolve the yeast and honey or molasses in the warm water. Combine the flours and yeast liquid, to form a firm dough and knead well on a floured board. Place the dough in a warm place in a bowl covered with a warm damp cloth for about 1 hour (or until doubled in size), then knead it again and shape it into 3 long loaves. Sprinkle over the caraway seeds. Place these loaves on a greased baking tray, cover with a warm damp cloth and again leave in a warm place until the loaves double in size (about 1 hour).

While the loaves are rising, preheat the oven to 425°F (220°C, gas mark 7). When the loaves are risen, bake them in the oven for 40 minutes. Remove from the oven and allow to cool on a wire rack.

LYN'S ORANGE AND HAZELNUT TEA BREAD
Makes a 2 lb (1 kg) loaf

6 oz (175 g) hazelnuts	6 oz (175 g) 81 per cent wholemeal flour
1 large orange	1 teaspoon baking powder
8 oz (225 g) cottage cheese	1 tablespoon (15 ml) clear honey
6 oz (225 g) brown sugar	
3 eggs, beaten	

Preheat oven to 350°F (175°C, gas mark 4). Reserve a few of the hazelnuts whole for decoration and chop up the rest. Cut two thin strips of rind from the orange and cut away any pith attached to them. Reserve these for decoration. Grate the remainder of the rind. Put the cottage cheese and sugar into a bowl and beat until creamy. Add the eggs and grated orange rind and beat again. Sift the flour and baking powder together and fold into the mixture. Stir in the chopped hazelnuts and put the mixture into a greased 2 lb (1 kg) bread tin. Bake in the preheated oven for 70–80 minutes, until nicely risen and golden brown on top. If the bread is correctly cooked the top will spring back when pressed. Turn the bread out of the tin and leave to cool on a wire rack. Meanwhile cut the reserved strips of orange rind into shreds and place in a small saucepan, just cover with water and gently boil for 5 minutes. Drain and mix the softened shreds of rind with the honey. Brush top of tea bread with this mixture, decorate with the reserved hazelnuts and leave to cool completely.

SLIGHTLY SWEET WHOLEMEAL FRUIT BREAD
Makes a 1½ lb (700 g) loaf

1 oz fresh yeast or 2 level
   teaspoons dry yeast

2 fl oz (50 g) warm water

4 oz (100 g) honey or brown sugar

1 lb (450 g) 81 per cent
   wholemeal flour

2 teaspoons salt

4 oz (100 g) sultanas or currants

2 tablespoons (30 ml) vegetable oil

16 fl oz (450 ml) warm water

Mix the yeast, warm water and honey into a smooth paste and leave the mixture to stand in a warm place for about 15–20 minutes or until frothed up. Combine the flour, salt, dried fruit and oil and mix thoroughly. Stir in the yeast mixture and slowly add the warm water to form a quite soft dough. Turn the dough onto a floured board and knead for 2–3 minutes. Place the dough in a clean bowl, cover with a warm damp cloth, set in a warm place and leave to rise for 1½-2 hours. Grease a 1½ lb (700 g) bread tin and press the dough into it. Cover with a warm damp cloth and leave to rise again for 45 minutes to 1 hour.

While the loaf is rising, preheat oven to 350°F (175°C, gas mark 4). When risen, bake the bread for 50 minutes or until it forms a nice golden brown crust. Turn onto a wire rack and leave to cool.

WALNUT, ALMOND AND RICE LOAF
Makes a 1½ lb (700 g) loaf

This is a versatile recipe, handy for using up left-over cooked vegetables, grains or beans (see *Variations* below).

8 oz (225 g) walnuts, finely chopped	1 medium carrot, grated
8 oz (225 g) almonds, finely chopped	1 teaspoon thyme
	1 tablespoon (15 ml) chopped fresh parsley
8 oz (225 g) cooked rice	4 oz (100 g) water, stock or milk
2 eggs, beaten	salt and black pepper to taste
2 oz (50 g) breadcrumbs	

Preheat oven to 375°F (190°C, gas mark 5). Combine all the ingredients and mix well. Turn mixture into a greased 1½ lb (700 g) bread tin and bake for 30 minutes or until a knife pushed into the centre of the loaf comes out clean. Serve hot or cold.

Variations
1 Add up to 1 lb (450 g) chopped cooked vegetables.
2 Add up to ½ lb (225 g) lightly sautéed mushrooms.
3 Add 8 oz (225 g) cooked beans or cooked grains.
4 Experiment with combinations of nuts other than those suggested.

HERB SCONES   *Makes 8-10*

These scones are good on their own and very tasty placed on
top of vegetable casseroles instead of dumplings.

8 oz (225 g) self-raising 81 per cent wholemeal flour	2 tablespoons (30 ml) chopped fresh herbs or 1 teaspoon dried mixed herbs
4 oz (100 g) vegetable margarine	pinch of salt
	water to mix

Preheat the oven to 425°F (215°C, gas mark 8). Rub the
margarine into the flour, add the herbs, salt and enough water
to mix to a soft dough. Roll out to ¾ in (1½ cm) thickness on
a floured board and cut into 2 in (5 cm) diameter rounds. Place
these on a greased baking sheet and bake in the preheated oven
for 10–12 minutes. Serve hot, spread with margarine or
sunflower seed spread.

QUICK PIZZA SANDWICH   *Serves 1*

This is a quick and convenient alternative to shop–bought pizza.

1 pitta bread	salt and freshly ground black pepper
1 large tomato, sliced	olives
2 oz (50 g) cheese, grated	½ teaspoon dried oregano

Preheat the oven to 450°F (230°C, gas mark 8). Cut the pitta
bread around the circumference so that you can open it up as
two circles joined by a hinge of bread. Layer one side with the
tomato slices, cover these with the grated cheese and season with
salt and black pepper. Decorate with the olives, sprinkle on the
oregano and then fold the empty half of the bread over the top.
Bake in the hot oven for 5 minutes or until the cheese has
melted. Serve immediately.

LYN'S SAVOURY SLICES   *Makes 12 slices*

Although vegetarian, these savoury slices are enjoyed by everyone. They are useful for buffets and packed lunches, as well as for lunch or dinner.

2 oz (50 g) vegetable margarine	1 egg, beaten
1 finely chopped onion	1 clove garlic, crushed (optional)
4 oz (100 g) mushrooms, chopped (optional)	1 tablespoon (15 ml) soya sauce
5 oz (125 g) rolled oats	1 tablespoon (15 ml) tomato sauce or purée
6 oz (150 g) finely grated carrot	1 teaspoon basil
5 oz (125 g) grated cheese	salt and black pepper to taste

Preheat oven to 325°F (170°C, gas mark 3). Melt the margarine in a pan and gently sauté the onion and mushrooms for 5 minutes. Transfer them to a mixing bowl and add all the other ingredients. Season to taste with salt and pepper and mix well. Press mixture into a greased baking tin and bake for 25-30 minutes. Cut into squares.

DATE AND OAT SLICES   *Makes 12 slices*

This recipe can be made with other dried fruits. The baked slices look wholesome and delicious and they are excellent for weaning children off commercial cakes and biscuits.

8 oz (225 g) 81 per cent wholemeal flour	6 oz (175 g) soft vegetable margarine
1 teaspoon cinnamon	8 oz (225 g) dates, stoned and chopped
½ teaspoon baking powder	5 fl oz (150 ml) water
4 oz (100 g) rolled oats	juice of ½ lemon
2 oz (50g) soft brown sugar	

Sift the flour, cinnamon and baking powder together. Return any separated bran to the mix and then stir in the oats. Rub in the margarine and stir in the sugar. Press half this mixture into a greased baking tin. Reserve the other half of the mixture. Preheat oven to 400°F (200°C, gas mark 6).

Simmer the dates in the water and lemon juice for 5 minutes. Cover the oat mixture in the tin with the date mixture and top it with the remaining oat mixture. Bake for 20-25 minutes in the preheated oven. Remove from the oven, cut into slices and then leave to cool in the tin. Store unused date and oat slices in an airtight tin.

SAVOURY OAT SLICES   *Makes 12 slices*

Serve these on their own or with a sauce (see pages 196 to 200).

2 oz (50 g) vegetable margarine	1 egg, beaten
1 medium onion, finely chopped	1 clove garlic, crushed
4 oz (100 g) mushrooms, chopped	1 tablespoon (15 ml) soya sauce
5 oz (150 g) rolled oats	1 tablespoon (15 ml) tomato purée
6 oz (175 g) carrot, finely grated	1 teaspoon dried basil
5 oz (150 g) cheese, grated	salt and black pepper to taste

Preheat oven to 350°F (180°C, gas mark 4). Melt the margarine in a pan and gently sauté the onion and mushrooms for 5 minutes. Transfer them to a mixing bowl and add all the other ingredients. Season to taste with salt and pepper and mix well. Press the mixture into a greased baking tin and bake for 20 minutes. Remove from the hot oven and allow to cool a little before cutting into slices. Serve hot or cold.

OATMEAL SCONES   *Makes 10-12*

4 oz (100 g) 81 per cent wholemeal flour	2 teaspoons baking powder
2 oz (50 g) butter or margarine	1 tablespoon (15 ml) honey or sugar (optional)
4 oz (100 g) fine oatmeal	about 2 fl oz (50 ml) milk

Preheat oven to 375°F (190°C, gas mark 5). Rub the butter or margarine into the flour and stir in the oatmeal. Add the remaining ingredients including enough milk to form a fairly stiff dough. Roll out to ½ in (1.25 cm) thickness on a floured board and cut into 2 in (5 cm) diameter rounds. Place these on a greased baking sheet and bake for 15 minutes or until nicely browned.

CHEESE AND OAT FINGERS   *Makes 12*

Prepare these oat fingers ahead of time and use them as required for snacks.

3 oz (75 g) 100 per cent wholemeal flour	4 oz (100 g) Cheddar cheese, grated
4 oz (100 g) rolled oats	salt and black pepper to taste
2 oz (50 g) finely chopped nuts (for example, walnuts, peanuts, hazelnuts etc)	1 egg, beaten
	2 oz (50 g) melted butter
1 tablespoon (15 ml) finely chopped parsley	3 tablespoons (45 ml) water

Combine the flour, oats, nuts, parsley, cheese and salt and black pepper to taste in a mixing bowl or the container of a food processor and mix well together. Beat together the egg, butter and water and stir it into the flour, nut, cheese and oat mixture. Preheat oven to 375°F (190°C, gas mark 5). Press the mixture evenly into a lightly greased baking tin and bake in the preheated oven for 30 minutes or until lightly browned. Remove from the oven, cool for a few minutes and then cut into fingers. Allow to cool completely and then store in an air-tight tin.

MUESLI TEA BREAD

Makes 2 × 1 lb (450 g) loaves

Bake ahead of time and use as required. It keeps for 3 or 4 days in a dry bread tin.

1 oz (25 g) fresh yeast or 3 teaspoons (15 ml) dried yeast	5 oz (150 g) sugar-free muesli
1 teaspoon molasses or honey	1 teaspoon salt
6 fl oz (175 ml) milk, diluted with 6 fl oz (175 ml) water, warmed	2 oz (50 g) soft vegetable margarine
1 lb (450 g) 81 per cent wholemeal flour	

Dissolve the yeast and molasses or honey in the milk solution. Combine the flour, muesli and salt in a warm bowl. Rub in the margarine and add the milk mixture and mix well to form a soft dough. Knead on a floured board for 5 minutes, then put in a clean dry bowl and leave, covered with a warm damp cloth, in a warm place for 40 minutes or until doubled in size. Knead the dough again, then divide it between two 1 lb (450 g) greased loaf tins. Cover and again leave in a warm place until the dough reaches the top of the tins (30–40 minutes). Meanwhile preheat the oven to 400°F (200°C, gas mark 6) and when the dough has risen sufficiently, bake the loaves for 25–30 minutes. Remove the baked bread from the tins and leave to cool on a wire rack.

TOFU CHEESECAKE

Makes a 1½ lb (750 g) cake

This is a very nice cake that uses no dairy products. It is suitable for vegans and those on a low-fat diet.

7 oz (200 g) 81 per cent wholemeal flour	water
1 oz (25 g) soya flour	2 oz (50 g) dates, chopped
2 teaspoons cinnamon	3 tablespoons (45 ml) lemon juice
2 oz (50 g) soft margarine	11 oz (300 g) tofu (beancurd – see page 31)

½ teaspoon grated lemon rind

3 tablespoons (45 ml)
    concentrated apple juice

sugar-free blackcurrant jam for
    topping

Preheat the oven to 350°F (180°C, gas mark 4). Mix together in a large bowl the wholemeal flour, soya flour and cinnamon. Rub in the margarine and add about 4 fl oz (100 ml) water to mix to a softish dough. Roll this out and use to line the base of a greased 8 in (20 cm) cake tin. Prick with a fork and then bake for 10 minutes in the hot oven. Meanwhile, simmer the dates in 2 fl oz (50 ml) water and the lemon juice for 5 minutes. Put the dates and liquid into a blender with the tofu, lemon rind and apple juice. Blend for 1 minute or until smooth. Pour this mixture over the baked pastry base in the cake tin and bake for about 20 minutes at 350°F (180°C, gas mark 4) or until the filling is set. Remove the cake from the oven, release it from the tin and top with a thin spreading of sugar–free blackcurrant jam.

CARROT CAKE   *Makes a 1½ lb (750 g) cake*

4 oz (100 g) soft vegetable
    margarine

3 oz (75 g) Barbados sugar

4 oz (100 g) carrot, finely grated

grated rind of 1 orange

8 oz (225 g) 81 per cent self-
    raising wholemeal flour

1 teaspoon baking powder

2 teaspoons cinnamon

TOPPING
2 oz (50 g) creamed coconut

juice of 1 orange or 2 fl oz
    (50 ml) orange juice

Preheat the oven to 350°F (180°C, gas mark 4). Cream the margarine together with the sugar until light and fluffy. Stir in the carrots and orange rind. Fold in the flour, baking powder and cinnamon. Mix thoroughly, then transfer the mixture to a greased 6 in (15 cm) cake tin with a circle of greaseproof paper in the base. Bake for 1 hour in the preheated oven. Release the cake from the tin and leave to cool on a wire rack. Meanwhile prepare the topping by melting the coconut over a low heat, then stirring in the orange juice. Spread this mixture evenly over the cooled cake.

CAROB CAKE   *Makes a 2 lb (900 g) cake*

The carob or locust bean is a legume and grows on evergreen trees common in the Mediterranean area. The ripe beans are sweet and dark brown in colour and provide a good substitute for cocoa when dried and powdered. Carob powder is sold as a health food replacement for cocoa because it does not contain caffeine and is soothing for upset stomachs.

4 oz (100 g) soft vegetable margarine	2 oz (50 g) 81 per cent self-raising wholemeal flour
4 oz (100 g) sugar	2 oz (50 g) ground almonds
4 eggs, separated	walnut halves for decoration
2 oz (50 g) carob powder	

FILLING AND TOPPING

3 oz (75 g) butter	1 tablespoon (15 ml) carob powder
4 oz (100 g) icing sugar	1 tablespoon (15 ml) boiling water

Preheat the oven to 350°F (180°C, gas mark 4). Lightly grease two 7 in (18 cm) sandwich tins. Beat the margarine and sugar together until creamy and fluffy and then slowly beat in the egg yolks. In a separate bowl, whisk the egg whites until stiff. Combine the carob powder, flour and almonds together and mix well. Stir half this mixture into the creamed margarine and sugar and then fold in the egg whites. Add the remaining carob mixture and gently stir. Divide the cake mix equally between the two tins and place them in the preheated oven. Bake for 20 minutes or until the cakes are firm and just springy to the touch. Turn the cakes out onto a wire tray and set aside to cool.

To make the filling and topping, cream the butter and icing sugar together until well blended, then beat in the carob powder and the boiling water. Use a third of this mixture to sandwich together the two halves of the cake. Place the cake on a serving plate and spread the remaining mixture evenly over the top.

GOOSEBERRY POUND CAKE
Makes a 1½ lb (700 g) loaf

Serve warm or cold with thick cream or yoghurt.

4 oz (100 g) butter	1½ teaspoons orange water or rose water
6 oz (175 g) 81 per cent self-raising wholemeal flour	1½ teaspoons aniseed or star anise, ground
4 oz (100 g) caster sugar	⅓ nutmeg, grated
2 egg yolks	4 oz (100 g) gooseberries, topped and tailed
1 tablespoon (15 ml) dry white wine	

Preheat oven to 350°F (180°C, gas mark 4). Thoroughly grease a 1½ lb (700 g) loaf tin. Melt the butter and when it is warm, but not hot, stir in the flour, sugar, egg yolks, wine, orange or rose water, aniseed and nutmeg. Combine well and beat until the mixture is light and fluffy. Spread half the mixture into the greased loaf tin. Top this with all the gooseberries keeping them from contact with the sides of the tin and cover these with the remaining cake mixture. Bake on the middle shelf of the preheated oven for 40–45 minutes or until the top is golden brown and a skewer pushed into the middle comes out clean. Allow to cool slightly before turning out of the tin.

DESSERTS

BANANA FANS   *Serves 4*

4 ripe but firm bananas, peeled	1 tablespoon (15 ml) clear honey
1 oz (25 g) butter or vegetable margarine	thick yoghurt or creme frâiche to taste
juice of 1 orange	ground cinnamon to taste

Slice each banana three times lengthwise to within 1 in (2.5 cm) of one end. Melt the margarine or butter over a low light and add the orange juice and honey. Slightly fan out the bananas and fry each one for 2–3 minutes in the melted fat, honey and orange juice. Turn once during cooking. Serve the bananas on warmed plates with a topping of yoghurt or creme frâiche and a sprinkling of cinnamon.

ROSE-FLAVOURED APPLES   *Serves 4*

This dessert is refreshing and cooling on a hot summer's day.

1 lb (450 g) eating apples, cored	ground cinnamon
juice of 1 lemon	crushed ice or ice cream or chilled yoghurt
2 oz (50 g) caster sugar	
2 tablespoons (30 ml) rose water	

Grate the apples into a mixing bowl, stir in the lemon juice, sugar and rose water. Transfer the mixture to individual serving bowls, dust with a little cinnamon and top with the crushed ice or ice cream or chilled yoghurt. Serve immediately.

SEMOLINA HALVA

Makes 2 lb (1 kg)

This is an Indian sweet. It makes an excellent dessert.

1 pint (550 ml) water	1 oz (25 g) almonds, blanched and chopped
4 oz (100 g) white or brown sugar	
4 oz (100 g) butter	1 oz (25 g) raisins
4 oz (100 g) semolina	

Bring the water to a boil, pour in the sugar and boil until it is all dissolved. Melt the butter in a frying pan or heavy saucepan over a moderate heat, add the semolina and cook, stirring continuously. As the semolina starts to brown, add the almonds and raisins and cook a further few minutes. Carefully pour in the sugar solution and cook, stirring, until the semolina is thick and doesn't stick to the sides of the pan. Pour into a shallow dish and allow to cool. Cut into squares while still just warm.

SWEET MOROCCAN COUSCOUS

Serves 4-6

12 dates, stoned	2 oz (50 g) currants
12 whole almonds, blanched	4 oz (100 g) sugar
8 oz (225 g) couscous	juice of 1 orange
10 fl oz (275 ml) hot water	1 oz (25 g) icing sugar
2 oz (50 g) butter, melted	2 teaspoons ground cinnamon
4 oz (225 g) mixed nuts finely chopped	

Stuff each of the dates with an almond and set aside. Put the couscous in a bowl and stir in the hot water. Set aside for 10 minutes. Then tip the couscous into a colander or seive, place this over a pan of boiling water and steam the couscous for 15 minutes. Rub the melted butter into the couscous and then steam it for a further 15 minutes. Place the couscous in a large bowl. Combine the chopped nuts, currants, sugar and orange juice in a separate bowl and then fold this mixture into the couscous. Pile on to a serving dish in a mound and decorate the top with the almond–stuffed dates. Sprinkle with icing sugar and cinnamon before serving.

FRESH FRUIT COMPOTE   *Serves 4*

The combination of fruit given in this recipe is only a suggestion. You may substitute any mixture of fruits.

4 oz (100 g) sugar	8 oz (225 g) strawberries, washed
12 fl oz (350 ml) water	2 sticks cinnamon or 1 teaspoon ground cinnamon
2 peaches, peeled	juice of 1 lemon
2 tart apples, washed	
8 oz (225 g) plums, washed, stoned, halved	

Put the sugar and water in a pan and bring to the boil. Set to simmer. Slice the skinned peaches and the apples and put them into the simmering syrup. Add the plums, strawberries, cinnamon and lemon juice. Simmer for 15 minutes, stirring occasionally. Remove the cinnamon sticks (if used). Serve hot or cold with whipped cream or natural yoghurt.

Variations
If rose water is available, add 1 or 2 drops to the simmering fruit. Try cardamom in place of the cinnamon for a different flavour.

FRUIT AND ALMOND
CHARLOTTE   *Serves 4-6*

1½ oz (40 g) soft brown sugar	1½ oz (40 g) raisins, washed
5 oz (125 g) wholemeal breadcrumbs	juice of ½ lemon
3 oz (75 g) ground almonds	1 teaspoon (5 ml) natural almond essence
grated rind of ½ lemon	
1 lb (450 g) cooking apples, thinly sliced	1 oz (25 g) soft vegetable margarine

Combine the sugar, breadcrumbs, ground almonds and lemon rind together and mix well. Preheat the oven to 350°F (180°C, gas mark 4). Make the following layers in a greased deep baking dish: apples, raisins, breadcrumb mixture, apples, raisins and finally breadcrumb mixture. Combine the lemon juice and almond essence and sprinkle it over the top. Finally, dot the top with knobs of margarine and bake in the preheated oven, covered, for 25 minutes. Remove the cover and bake for a further 15 minutes. Serve.

BAKED APPLES   *Serves 4*

This is quick to prepare and then convenient to leave to bake while you get on with other jobs.

4 Bramley cooking apples, cored	4 dates, stoned
3 tablespoons (45 ml) sultanas or currants or a mixture of both	2 tablespoons (30 ml) maple syrup or ordinary syrup or honey
1 tablespoon (15 ml) chopped walnuts	

Preheat the oven to 375°F (190°C, gas mark 5). Wash the apples and place them on a greased baking tray. Stuff them with a mixture of the sultanas (or currants) and nuts. Plug each apple with a date and cover with maple syrup or honey. Bake for 20–25 minutes in the hot oven. Serve immediately with natural yoghurt or whipped cream.

PINEAPPLE AND YOGHURT ICE   *Serves 4*

Desserts such as this one, which can be made in advance and removed from the deep freeze at a moment's notice, are most convenient. This recipe also offers a way of making use of a ripe pineapple which is perhaps not needed immediately or which was bought cheaply because of its near over-ripeness.

1 medium size ripe pineapple	1-2 tablespoons white rum or kirsch
5 oz (150 g) clear honey	
1 lb (450 g) thick Greek style yoghurt	

Peel the pineapple and remove the central core. Purée half the pineapple in a blender and chop the remainder. Place all the pineapple in a saucepan with the honey and bring to the boil. Reduce the heat and simmer for 10 minutes. Cool. Stir in the yoghurt and white rum or kirsch. Freeze in a shallow freezer-proof dish for 1 hour, then beat until smooth. Re-freeze. Take out of the freezer about 10–15 minutes before serving. Serve in scoops in sundae dishes.

PLUMS IN SPICED CUSTARD   *Serves 4*

The custard in this recipe is made with yoghurt, eggs and honey.

1 lb (450 g) ripe plums, halved and stoned	¼ teaspoon mixed spice
6 fl oz (175 ml) natural yoghurt	¼ teaspoon ground cinnamon
2 tablespoons (30 ml) clear honey	2 tablespoons (30 ml) flaked almonds
2 large eggs, separated	

Preheat the oven to 180°C (350°F, gas mark 4). Put the plums in a single layer in a lightly greased, shallow, ovenproof dish.

Beat the yoghurt with the honey, egg yolks, mixed spice and cinnamon. Whisk the egg whites until stiff but not dry and fold into the yoghurt mixture. Spoon this evenly over the plums and sprinkle with the flaked almonds. Stand the dish in a roasting tin and pour enough hot water into the roasting tin to come halfway up the side of the dish. Bake in the preheated oven for 35–40 minutes. Serve hot.

APRICOT FUDGE   *Makes 1 lb (450 g)*

Apricots have been used in this recipe, but you may substitute the same weight of other dried fruits.

2 oz (50 g) dried apricots, finely chopped	4 fl oz (100 ml) water
3 oz (75 g) plain chocolate	2 oz (50 g) clear honey
12 oz (350 g) sugar	4 oz (100 g) butter

Put all the ingredients into a saucepan with a heavy base. Stir over a low light until the butter has melted, the sugar has dissolved and the mixture is homogeneous. Raise the heat a little and bring the mixture to the boil. If you have a kitchen thermometer, boil the mixture until it reaches 240°F (115°C). If you do not have a thermometer, boil to the soft–ball stage (at this stage a drop of the boiling liquid, dripped into cold water, will set but should remain soft when pressed). Now remove the pan from the heat and leave it for 5 minutes. Meanwhile grease a baking tin 9 in × 6 in (22 cm × 15 cm) or one of different dimensions but the same area. Beat the cooked mixture with a wooden spoon until it starts to look grainy and then pour it into the tin. Put the tin aside for the fudge to set. When set, cut into squares and serve. Store unused fudge in an airtight tin.

PASHKA

Serves 6-8

This is a traditional Russian Easter pudding. It is relatively quick and easy to make, but makes an impressive finale to a special meal. Serve with macaroons or *langue de chat* biscuits.

1 egg yolk	2 oz (50 g) raisins
2 oz (50 g) soft brown sugar	2 oz (50 g) almonds, chopped and toasted
1 lb (450 g) curd cheese	
grated rind and juice of 1 orange	5 fl oz (150 ml) whipping cream
2 oz (50 g) glacé cherries, quartered	½ teaspoon ground cinnamon

Beat the egg yolk and sugar to a thick cream. Add the cheese and beat well, to remove any lumps. Mix the orange juice and rind, the cherries, the raisins and the almonds into this. Whip the cream until stiff, then fold it gently into the cheese and fruit mixture. Line a 1¾ pint (generous 1 litre) pudding basin with a piece of muslin large enough to overlap the top. Spoon in the pashka mixture and fold the overlapping muslin over this. Cover with a saucer and place a 1 lb (450 g) weight on top. Chill overnight in the refrigerator. To serve, remove the saucer and weight, unfold the muslin invert onto a serving plate and remove the muslin. Sprinkle with cinnamon and serve.

NUTTY PEAR CRUMBLE

Serves 4-6

This is a simple but very popular dessert. It looks appetizing and the chopped nuts in the crumble give it an interesting texture. Serve with natural yoghurt or cream. The same recipe can be used to make apple, apricot or any other stewed fruit crumble.

6 large dessert pears	5 oz (150 g) butter
2 tablespoons (30 ml) clear honey	4 oz (100 g) dark brown sugar
4 fl oz (100 ml) water	3 oz (75 g) coarsely chopped hazelnuts
8 oz (225 g) wholemeal flour	

Preheat the oven to 350°F (180°C, gas mark 4). Peel, core and thickly slice the pears. Put the pears, honey and water in a pan, bring to a gentle boil, reduce heat, cover and simmer for 5 minutes or until the pears are just tender. Stir occasionally. Transfer the pears to a shallow baking dish and arrange them neatly in the bottom. Pour over them the honey syrup from the pan. Rub the flour and butter together in a mixing bowl to form a crumble with the texture of coarse breadcrumbs (alternatively use a food processor to do the job). Stir in the sugar and hazelnuts and spread the crumble evenly over the top of the pears. Bake in the preheated oven for 45 minutes or until nicely browned. Serve hot or cold.

APPLE, BANANA AND LEMON DESSERT
Serves 4

4 oz (100 g) sugar	2 bananas, peeled and sliced
6 fl oz (175 ml) water	peel of 2 lemons, grated
4 tart apples, peeled, cored and sliced	juice of 2 lemons
	2 teaspoons ground cinnamon

Put the sugar and water into a heavy pan and bring to the boil. Add the apples, bananas, lemon peel, lemon juice and cinnamon. Simmer until nearly all the liquid has evaporated and the mixture is thick (about 15 minutes). Serve hot or cold, with natural yoghurt, garnished with toasted almonds.

APRICOT RICE PUDDING *Serves 4*

This recipe uses dried apricots, but fresh ones, when available, can be substituted. With dried apricots, serve the rice pudding hot as a warming autumn or winter dessert. With fresh apricots serve the pudding chilled.

8 oz (225 g) dried apricots, chopped	1 pint (550 ml) milk
2 tablespoons apricot jam	½ teaspoon nutmeg
6 oz (175 g) short grain brown rice	grated rind of 1 lemon

Place the apricots in a saucepan and cover with boiling water. Cover the pan and cook the apricots for about 40 minutes over a low heat until soft. Drain, if necessary. Stir the jam into the cooked apricots. Place the rice in a saucepan with a well-fitting lid and add the milk, nutmeg and lemon rind and simmer over a low heat for about 40 minutes or until the rice is cooked and all the milk absorbed. Pile the rice into the centre of a serving dish, pour the apricots over the rice and serve.

HEALTHY BANANA DELIGHT *Serves 4*

This can literally be whipped together in minutes. It is a great favourite with children.

2 large bananas, sliced	2 tablespoons (30 ml) milk
1 tablespoon (15 ml) wheatgerm	juice of 1 orange
1 tablespoon (15 ml) ground almonds	1 tablespoon (15 ml) concentrated apple juice

Put all the ingredients into a liquidizer and blend for about ½ minute. Distribute between four fruit bowls and serve.

APRICOT SWIRL

Serves 4

In this dessert, a tangy fruit purée is married with creamy fromage frais.

8 oz (225 g) dried apricots	8 oz (225 g) fromage frais
5 fl oz (150 ml) unsweetened orange juice	1 tablespoon (15 ml) clear honey

Soak the apricots in the orange juice, overnight preferably, but for at least 4 hours. Bring to the boil, then simmer gently for 15 minutes. Purée the apricots with any remaining juice in a liquidizer or food processor and leave to cool. Stir the honey into the fromage frais and put it into a serving dish. Spoon in the apricot purée and fold gently into the fromage frais to give a marbled appearance. Serve chilled.

MOLASSES APPLE CAKE

Makes a 2 lb (1 kg) cake

6 oz (175 g) cooking apples, thinly sliced	4 oz (100 g) sugar
¾ lb (325 g) molasses	1 teaspoon cinnamon
3 oz (75 g) butter	½ teaspoon cloves
5 fl oz (125 ml) hot water	¼ teaspoon nutmeg
12 oz (300 g) 81 per cent wholemeal flour	1 level tablespoon (15 ml) baking powder
	¼ teaspoon salt

Preheat oven to 350°F (180°C, gas mark 4). Cook the apples in the molasses over a low heat until tender. Leave to cool. Melt the butter in the hot water. Sift the flour, sugar, spices, baking powder and salt together and gradually add the hot water and butter mixture, stirring constantly to keep smooth. Stir in molasses and apple mixture. Poured into a greased baking tin. Bake in the preheated oven for about 30 minutes. Serve warm.

RHUBARB PUDDING　　　　　*Serves 4*

This is a thick layer of rhubarb, perfumed with orange and topped with a soft batter lid.

1 lb (450 g) rhubarb	grated rind and juice of 1 large orange
½ teaspoon ground ginger	2 tablespoons (30 ml) soft brown sugar
2 tablespoons (30 ml) raisins	

BATTER

11 oz (300 g) wholemeal flour	2 eggs
pinch of salt	1 pint (500 ml) milk
4 oz (100 g) soft brown sugar	

Preheat the oven to 350°F (180°C, gas mark 4). Wash, trim and slice the rhubarb and cover the bottom of a fireproof dish with it. Mix the sugar, orange rind, raisins and ginger together. Sprinkle this over the fruit then pour over the orange juice.

Combine the batter ingredients and beat or whisk into a smooth batter. Pour it over the rhubarb. Bake in the preheated oven for 1 hour, then serve.

ENGLISH-AMERICAN FOOD AND COOKING TERMS

FOOD

English	American
castor sugar	granulated white sugar
demerara	dark brown sugar
icing sugar	confectioners sugar
treacle	molasses
biscuit	cooky or cracker
scone	biscuit
porridge	oatmeal
currant	raisin
french bean	snap or string bean
swede	rutabaga
spring onions	scallions
courgettes	zucchini
marrow	squash
cornflour	cornstarch
aubergine	egg plant

COOKING

to grill	to broil
to ice	to frost
to mince	to grind
tin	can
baking tin	cake pan
baking sheet	cookie sheet
frying pan	skillet

OVEN TEMPERATURES

Temperature gauge	Oven temperature °F	Oven temperature °C	Gas mark
very low to low	200–300	93–148	¼, ½, 1, 2
medium low to med	300–350	148–176	3
moderate	350–375	176–190	4
medium high to high	375–450	190–232	5, 6, 7
very high	450–500	232–315	8, 9

CONVERSION OF IMPERIAL MEASUREMENTS TO METRIC

The following table may be used for the conversion of imperial to metric:

Ounces/fluid ounces	Grams or millilitres (to nearest unit of 25)
1	25
2	50
3	75
4	100
5	150
6	175
7	200
8	225
9	250
10	275
11	300
12	350
13	375
14	400
15	425
16	450
17	475
18	500
19	550
20	575

ENGLISH-AMERICAN MEASUREMENTS

English   *American*

fluid

1 pint = 20 fl oz   1 pint = 16 fl oz
2 pints = 1 quart = 40 fl oz   2 pints = 1 quart = 32 fl oz
1 fl oz   1½ tablespoons

dry measures

flour
1 oz   4 tablespoons (¼ cup)
2 oz   8 tablespoons (½ cup)
4 oz   1 cup

butter, sugar
1 oz   2 tablespoons
2 oz   4 tablespoons (¼ cup)
8 oz   1 cup

INDEX